TO SONIE:

Your support of my book from the beginning means more to me than you will ever know. I will always appreciate your encouragement and advice. Thank you Sonie.

Jack Gangstad

From Diapers to Diplomas

A Common Sense Approach to Raising Well-adjusted Children

by

Jack Gangstad

Bloomington, IN

Milton Keynes, UK

AuthorHouse™
1663 Liberty Drive, Suite 200
Bloomington, IN 47403
www.authorhouse.com
Phone: 1-800-839-8640

AuthorHouse™ UK Ltd.
500 Avebury Boulevard
Central Milton Keynes, MK9 2BE
www.authorhouse.co.uk
Phone: 08001974150

First published by AuthorHouse 6/27/2006

ISBN: 1-4259-4345-4 (sc)

Library of Congress Control Number: 2006905387

Printed in the United States of America
Bloomington, Indiana

This book is printed on acid-free paper.

Table of Contents

Dedicated to

Deb: There have been other mothers as good as you, but none better. Through your influence, I became a better father.

Sarah: I do not think I would have made this commitment without your consistent support. You kept telling me, "Dad, you should write a book." Well Sarah, thanks in large part to you, we did it. I love you more than my words can possibly express.

Betsy: You are something special. You have brought happiness into our lives from the day you were born. We love you and are proud to call you our daughter.

Bob and Jewell Gangstad
Eric and Betty Clark: Deb and I could not have picked a better set of role models.

Introduction

> *A perfect parent is a person with excellent child-rearing theories and no actual children.* — *Dave Barry*

As I reflect on my own experience as a young parent, I must confess I was not very certain about what I was doing. My wife and I continually asked each other if we were making the right decisions concerning the upbringing of our two daughters. Our insecurity was compounded by the feeling that we were surrounded by parents who appeared to be so confident in how they were raising their kids. We would observe these parents and know we did not agree with some of their ideas. In hindsight, I realize we had our own parents to thank for these parental instincts. My wife and I were both blessed with wonderful role models.

Each time my wife asked, "Jack, do you think we are doing the right thing?" I would answer her by saying that we would find out in the next twenty years. I did not fully realize at the time what a helpful guide (**looking at the big picture**) that approach to parenting would turn out to be for both of us. It is ironic and sad that some of the parents who seemed back then to have all the answers have raised children who have met with a lot of difficulties.

We all make mistakes and I can assure you I made my fair share. Fortunately, my wife and I have been able to avoid the big errors some parents are guilty of. We recognize that much of the credit is due our parents, relatives, friends, teachers, and coaches who had a positive influence on our lives. The majority of our parenting skills are ideas we have taken from our role models. I now feel much different from the way I did many years ago when my apparently never-ending role as a parent began. I am more confident now. I certainly do not have all the answers, but I have learned many lessons that I hope will help young parents. It is said that a wise person learns from the mistakes of others. As a public school teacher and coach, friend, neighbor, and relative, I have seen many parents, with the best of intentions, make what I believe to be mistakes in raising their children. By having the opportunity to live in the same location all my life, I have been able to see the consequences of poor parenting. Many of the problems that surface in the teenage years can be traced back to faulty decisions made by parents when their children were young. I will share those errors in judgment and give you examples of how the children were affected. It is not easy being a parent or a child in today's society.

When people find out I am a high school teacher, one of the questions they usually ask is, "What is wrong with young people today? They seem to have so many problems." I tell them that there are still a lot of good kids in school. I go on to say that kids have not changed. **Parents have changed and families have changed.** These changes are having a negative effect on a growing number of children. If we do not return to many of the traditional parenting techniques of the past, our problems are going to continue to get worse. That is one of the reasons I am writing this book. In many ways, schools are only going to be as good as the quality of children in them. Today's parents must do a better job than my generation did.

There are certainly more ways than one to raise well-adjusted children. My suggestions are not going to work for everyone. I will share ideas that have worked for our family with the hope some of these concepts will help others. What I have learned may reassure young parents in their moments of uncertainty that they are taking the correct approach. These young parents will still have to wait until their children grow up to truly see how they have done. I think they will find it well worth the wait.

One of the most satisfying rewards in my life has been to see our two daughters be successful as young adults. Each time they received some type of honor or award, I was happy for them because they earned it themselves. My wife and I took satisfaction from the girls doing well because it reassured us: we must be doing something right as parents.

Among the most gratifying aspects of teaching is to have a student or parent write me a thank you note, invite me to a wedding or reunion, select me to write their letter of recommendation, make a contribution in my name to our Township Foundation, or come back to visit after they have graduated. I only mention these examples because I hope they give the ideas expressed in this book some credibility. I could not have written this manuscript twenty-five years ago. Hopefully, with age comes wisdom. Common sense is part of wisdom and one of the most important qualities a parent must possess. *From Diapers to Diplomas* is a proactive book containing common sense suggestions for raising children. Today, it seems common sense is uncommon.

One of my nephews went to high school with our daughters. He is a newlywed and I appreciated him taking the time to read my book and offer his reactions. In his e-mail he wrote, "As fundamental as the ideas and advice seem to you and I, the book depicts a pretty unique line of thinking for the rest of America, who neglect their children on a daily basis. My most obvious reaction to the book is that I agree with you. Your methods are correct, plain, and simple. It may sound vain to state, 'this is the way to parent,' but I wouldn't second guess you if you did write that at the start of the book. You have a special insight to many different types of children because you raised kids who attended public school in an upscale community, yet also teach at a large, more diverse public school closer to the urban city. Both of your daughters earned exceptional grades, yet were socially active and well-liked."

Part of parenting is on-the-job training. Raising children is hard work and it would be a mistake to believe that reading this book will magically transform newlyweds into effective parents. However, the lessons I have learned over the years are significant. I hope these suggestions can supplement the everyday experiences of parents to help them raise well-adjusted children.

Acknowledgements

If you have ever started a home repair project anticipating a two hour job and it turned into a marathon undertaking, you have some idea what it was like for me to write this book. For a professional author, the time and energy involved in crafting a book are predictably immense. However, for a rookie such as me, ignorance was bliss. If I had known what I do now back when I started the first chapter, I am not sure I would have made the commitment. Four summers ago I sat down in front of our home computer and started a mission I fully expected to finish by the end of the summer. More than four years have passed since that June morning.

As the months went by, I received support from many different people. At the risk of overlooking someone, I feel I should thank as many of these individuals as I can remember. If I did forget someone, please forgive me.

Sonie Bowers and Roger Davis patiently assisted me with their revision suggestions. I will always be grateful for their help with a neophyte author. Heidi Newman was a big help in the editing process. I valued Heidi's input and expertise.

Whenever I needed some encouragement and/or constructive criticism, there were several friends and colleagues who provided it. I remember their kind words during the times I wondered if I would ever finish my book. I want to thank Terry Feezle, Connie Hines, Mike Miley, Randy Racine, Dave Mock, Tim Ricker, Jeff Young, Tim Stone, Heather Branigan, Ann Hyer, and Colonel Mike Kelly. There are many others I would like to recognize including Mary Kay Overbeck, Maria O'Connor, Dan McGill, Pat Wiehe, Carl Gibson, Jackie Mock,

Mary Beth Reffett, Jim Alexander, Molly Clark, Nathan Miley, Fred Williams, Chuck Jones, Anita Walther, Paul Brown, Joanne Hughes, Leanne Kabrich, Nancy Racine, Susan Davis, Bob and Vicki Gangstad, David and Laura Gangstad, Mike and Kim Gangstad, Joe and Danielle Gangstad, Lynn Boatman, Jack Savant, Bruce Blomberg, Joe Murphy, DeeAnn Ramey, Sue Clark, Drew Clark, Todd Racine, Sherry Miley, Jay Hill, Paul and Kathy Loggan, Jack and Kathy Durkin, Carolynn Bobbitt, Brian Pritchard, Dick Pritchard, George Schneider, Jay Hamerstadt, Wayne Norlin, Ron and Faye Little, Nita Stout, Lynn Slivka, Marilyn Beeler, George Jackson, Mark Barnes, Basil Smotherman, Andy Wiggins, Rick Stover, Dan Howell, Ed Jones, Pam Williams, Jean Martin, Ron Hoppes, Joan Jacobs, Rick Shadiow, Jeremy Moore, Scott Bowen, Bill Naas, Jeff Nass, Jerry, Susan, Katie, and Jamie Haskett, Margo and Bill Finney, Chris Wolf, Carol and Jim Lehman, Sally Zimney, Jim Dyar, Chuck Poulsen, Loretta Connor, Betsy Laskey, Melanie Tolliver, Andy Murphy, Peter Brown, Ann Leonard, Carol Brown, Norm Bower, Kathy Serge, Roberta Quandt, Megan Lynch, Dave Calvert, Sue Landaw, Mark Shaw, Patti Mendenhall, Litzi Ploski, Jasmin Jordan, Jo and Randy Craig, Mike and Ginny Antrim, Karen Schneider, Julie Grissom, Leanne Haggard, Ginny Jutte, Jan Wendt, Steve Kappes, MJ Hamaker, Kelly Quiesser, Cindy W. Boatman, Jim Price, Matt Evans, Mary Wynne Cox, Sue Landaw, Bill Gulde, Inder and Nancy Jarial, Barbi Kern, John King, Rob Hendrix, Eugene White, Joe Erne, Taylor and Margot Clark, Kathy Ellis, Joyce Karrmann, Phil McIntyre, Chris Vermilion, Marc Anderson, Andy Noble, Lou Silverman, Sue Poulos, Cathy Muterspaugh, Amy Carson, Leslie Decker, and Dennis Neary. Finally, to the students of North Central High School who provided me with so many helpful ideas, I thank all of you.

When someone experiences success, there is usually more than one person responsible for that accomplishment. In the case of this book, each one of the people mentioned helped me and I want them to know how much I appreciate their support. Thank you.

— Jack Gangstad

As the twig is bent, so grows the tree.

Chapter One
The Formative Years

There are no guarantees when it comes to parenting. None of us knows what the next day or even hour will bring. We can only try to do our best. Even then, things may not turn out the way we expect. How can anyone explain a family with three children where two kids seem to be well-adjusted, while the third has the parents pulling out their hair? All three kids were raised by the same parents, but with very different results. Your responsibility as a parent is to provide all the love, guidance, and attention your children need. Then, as the children mature, they will make the decisions that will determine what kind of life they build for themselves.

It is no coincidence I begin this book about parenting by considering the child's formative years. This is the time when some parents make their biggest mistakes, while others build strong foundations for the future. I describe the formative years to be the time between conception and when the child starts elementary school. By age six, most children have begun making decisions on their own. The important formative years are when parents must do their best work. Unfortunately, it is a time when a growing number of them are dropping the ball. Many of these same parents will pay dearly for failing to invest the time, love, and energy needed during this critical period in the development of their child's personality.

Young children are like pieces of clay. To a large extent, you can mold them and shape them any way you choose. They will believe most things you tell them. During the formative years, in their eyes, you are the ultimate authority figure. Until about first grade, if they have a question, your answer will be accepted unconditionally. Then they start thinking for themselves. As parents, you have to make sure they are hearing the right words and absorbing the right ideas. If you do not provide this important guidance, who does? Any caregiver who parents select to fill in for them must be trustworthy and someone in whom they have complete confidence because once these years are past, they will not get a second chance. I cannot emphasize enough that it is during the pre-school years that parents must do their best work. If parents miss this opportunity, their failure will come back to haunt them later.

In this chapter I will discuss the following points:

- establishing priorities to allow parents the time to interact with their child
- education begins in the home and parents should be their child's first teacher
- instilling positive values, patriotism, love of reading, and respect for the property of others
- stimulating creativity
- the need for your child to play with other children
- protecting the innocence of childhood, and
- why parents should support each other in providing for the needs of their child.

A young child needs a loving, close, and nurturing relationship with an adult who is caring for a minimum number of other children. This caregiver-to-child ratio is important, because children should not have to compete with each other for the adult's attention. In our family, my wife and I agreed she would be that vital influence for our children. We are both teachers. Courses in educational psychology, along with child development, were an important part of our teacher training. The research we were taught demonstrated that the formative years are the time when the majority of a child's personality is formed. Many young parents underestimate the importance of these critical years.

Single parents generally have fewer choices concerning child care and undoubtedly have a more difficult job parenting. Without the support of a spouse, I am surprised single parents do as well as they do. I cannot imagine how difficult it would have been to raise our two children by myself. Many single parents are just trying to get by from day to day.

A contrast to the single-parent family is the dual-income family. I would define a dual-income family as one where both parents work and send their young children to be cared for by someone else for the majority of each working day. Remember, I expressed the view that every child needs someone to provide that consistent and special influence during the formative years. *I did not say it had to be the mother.* I know productive and well-adjusted young adults who have grown up with a mother and father who worked full-time during their formative years. These parents were able to find a loving grandparent (or other caring relative), a willing and able neighbor, or a high quality child care facility.

More and more kids are growing up with a lack of values, discipline, and direction. Children need parents to notice the things they do. Kids need to know they are more important to their parents than a new car, a vacation, or a big house. After listening to the comments of a growing number of my students, I worry that they place more value on material possessions than people.

The most important gift parents can give their children is time. For a few years, live in a smaller house. Drive an older car. Eat at home. Postpone the expensive vacations. I have heard working parents say they would like to stay home with their young children but cannot afford it. I am sure in many cases this is true. However, from my observation, some may be unwilling to make the sacrifices necessary to meet this important goal. I cannot help but think that in some of these cases, with *temporary* material sacrifices, one of the parents could stay home until the youngest child starts first grade. That parent could then resume his or her career, and both could enjoy the satisfaction of knowing they have built a strong foundation for their child's personality. **Parents need to have their priorities in order.** An excellent article that was in *Reader's Digest* helps make my point. Bob Greene titled his story, "A Father, a Son, and an Answer." He wrote:

> "There are parents who can afford to send their children to Europe or Disneyland, and the children turn out rotten. There are parents who live in million-dollar houses and give their children cars and swimming pools, yet something goes wrong. Rich and poor, black and white, so much goes wrong so often. The answer is so simple: parents who care enough to spend time, and to pay attention and try their best. It doesn't cost a cent, yet it is the most valuable thing in the world."

Hearing some parents talk about their kids, I do not know why they even had children. They do not appear to enjoy being around them. Whenever possible, they figure out ways to avoid spending time with them. It seems that some of these parents do not want to stay home with their children. They are not willing to invest the time, love, and energy required when it is needed the most. Inevitably, these parents do not like what they see in their older children. Kids sense this disapproval and seek attention by misbehaving. Unfortunately, by then it is too late to change most kids.

My wife stayed home with our two children for nine years. I can understand the financial concerns of young parents— our family knows the reality of living paycheck to paycheck. We made a number of adjustments that allowed us to make our decision work until our younger child started first grade. We babysat for families when the parents went away on business trips. We would move in with their children and stay in their homes. We would do this four to six weeks each year. The demand for this service is increasing, and the grapevine is very effective. We found it a good way to earn extra money. My wife cared for one additional child during the day which also supplemented our income and helped us pay the bills. I worked during the summers and coached several sports during the school year. People who sincerely want to do something can usually find a way to make it work. Was it hard? **Yes.** Did we sacrifice a significant amount? **Yes.** Was it worth it? **Yes.** We both agree we would do the same thing over again, regardless of the costs. **We have no regrets.**

As a high school teacher, one of the biggest differences I have noticed in my students from when I started in 1975 is the change in their values. A growing number of students are exhibiting disturbingly poor attitudes and habits such as:

- a lack of respect for authority
- a belief that the end justifies the means
- excessive materialism
- a belief that anything goes as long as you do not get caught
- a disregard for the truth
- drug abuse and the negative effects that follow
- poor work ethic
- sleep deprivation
- poor nutrition
- lack of pride

- lack of mental toughness
- inconsistency of effort and attendance
- apathy toward their education
- boredom in most areas of their lives
- lack of manners (rudeness)
- sexual promiscuity, and
- foul language.

Some of these same problems were, of course, around in 1975; however, attitudes are more negative today. We still have many good kids, but from my observation, a growing number of students are making bad decisions. I am convinced the majority of these troubles are a direct result of poor parenting.

My biggest illusion as a young teacher involved my desire to right wrongs. I thought that if I put my arm around kids with problems and said all the right things, they would turn their lives around. Fortunately, this has happened occasionally, which gives me great satisfaction. For the most part though, these kids will listen to me, give me all the right answers, then go right on making the same bad choices.

I use analogies when I teach. I compare working with young people to farming. You can be the best farmer in the state. You can have the best equipment, the best seeds, fertilizer, insecticides and even the best weather. However, if the soil in which you are growing your crops is of poor quality, none of the other things will be effective. The crops will fail. It is the same with students. They will have a difficult time in school if they do not have "fertile minds and personalities" which allow them to grow and learn. They simply will not develop properly. The best facilities and the newest computers will have minimal effect. Like the farmer who needs the right soil to grow his crops, students need the proper attitudes if they are to grow intellectually and emotionally. **Fertile minds and personalities are developed in the home.**

So, what should young parents do? It all begins with values. Sunday School and the influence of the church had a significant impact on the development of positive morals in our daughters. The most important influence will be you, as their role model. Actions speak louder than words. You cannot expect your kids to follow your advice and ignore your example. Those little eyes and ears take in much more than parents realize. In turn, your children's ideals will determine the decisions they make. The decisions they make will determine the quality of their lives.

One of my favorite activities when our children were young was reading to them at bedtime. The sooner parents start this routine the better, because even a newborn can begin the process of language acquisition. My wife always made sure we had available plenty of books appropriate for their age levels. On most nights, we let the girls choose the stories they wanted to hear. As they grew, once or twice a week, we would read one of *Aesop's Fables.* We would talk about the moral of the story. Reading followed by discussion is another way you can teach values to your children.

We would read to our kids almost every day. I particularly remember them enjoying the *Berenstein Bears* book and tape collection. Those stories were not just fun; they also presented real-life problems along with suggestions for solving them. We listened to the classic Walt Disney books with tapes. Even I enjoyed hearing those Disney stories—the same ones I had heard when I was growing up. It was not long at all before the girls were reading for themselves.

My parents and uncles served in the military during World War II. Listening to the stories of the sacrifices made by these war veterans taught me more about patriotism than any history book.

What about today's children? Young parents must make a conscious effort to ensure their kids develop the proper respect for our country and the sacrifices made by those who went before us. Parents must demonstrate patriotism to small children. They should teach their young children to stand and put their hands over their hearts when the National Anthem is played. Parents should help their kids learn the words to our National Anthem and Pledge of Allegiance.

Parents must set the example. It is difficult these days to get some of our high school students to stand and recite the Pledge of Allegiance. When our National Anthem is played, many kids continue talking to their friends and fail to take off their hats. Our schools should reinforce proper patriotic conduct. On the Fourth of July, take your children to the parades and fireworks displays. Talk with them about the significance of these celebrations. Even with our problems, this is the greatest country in the world. Our kids must be taught to respect and appreciate it.

Children must also be taught to respect and care for our environment. One way to do this is by not allowing your kids to litter. Teach them to put all trash in appropriate containers. When you go on a picnic or other outdoor activity, expect them to help clean up before you go home. Leave your area as clean as, or cleaner than, it was before you arrived. Try to recycle as much trash as possible. Kids can be taught to put aluminum cans and plastic in separate containers. They will notice when you put your old newspapers there, too. Your children can help take out the trash each week and see how much of it can be recycled. When you do these things over and over, kids will get the message.

Teach respect for the property of others. It is up to parents to initiate this process and for our schools to support it. I am frustrated when I see what students do to our school restrooms and locker rooms. They frequently throw their trash on the floor right next to the trash can. They throw litter in sinks, urinals, and toilets. They show no respect for our school, an attitude which stems from a lack of proper training. I have even caught students spitting on our floors and carpeting. Why do they do it? Many of our problems today could be solved if parents would inspire their children to live by the Golden Rule: do unto others as you would have others do unto you.

Stimulate creativity in your children. **Watching television should be kept to a minimum.** My wife and I had a room where we kept all the kids' things. There were crayons, markers, and plenty of paper. Kids love to draw pictures that tell stories. They will want to show you their artwork. Do not just look it over quickly and say, "Oh, that's nice." Sit down next to them. Put your arms around them and really look at what they have created on the paper. Observe all the little details. Some of them might not make sense to you, but each line is there for a reason. Ask questions about their drawings. Listen to their explanations. I suspect you will not be able to keep from smiling at their imaginations.

As I write these words, wonderful memories come back to me. My wife would attach the girls' pictures to the refrigerator with colorful magnets. I always loved seeing their faces light up when they came to visit me at my school and saw their masterpieces displayed on my office wall. I still have some of those pictures. I have saved them through the years and some day I will give them back to our daughters. I wonder how many parents miss out on these special moments because they are too busy or have other priorities. From experiences such as these, children receive clear messages of acceptance, importance, and love.

We also had toys and puzzles for the kids to play with. We collected stuffed animals, blocks, toy cars, trucks, and a big box full of clothes. The girls had a lot of fun dressing up and playing make-believe. Parents can occasionally join in their play. Get down on the floor and really interact with your kids. They make some of the cutest, funniest, most imaginative comments as they play with all these different toys.

Our first house was small and our daughters shared a bedroom. We painted the alphabet on one wall along with a picture of something which started with the first letter (A—apple, B— Balloon, etc.). Above their closet we painted the numbers 0-1-2-3-4-5-6-7-8-9-10. All of these were done in different colors—another way to introduce letters and numbers as well as brighten up their room. I can remember hearing our older daughter using the figures on the bedroom walls to teach her little sister. She was obviously imitating her mother. Who knows how much the older child taught the younger? I believe it was a significant amount.

Kids are smart— much smarter than some adults give them credit for. When each of our girls was around 15 months, my wife began working on colors, letters, numbers, names, and objects. I remember her using m & m's and dyed Easter eggs to teach colors. We had a toy called a Magna-Doodle that was great for drawing and reviewing both letters and numbers. All parents need to do is look around and use their imaginations. It will be satisfying to you, as your child's first teacher, to see your child learn and grow. **Education begins in the home.**

You do not need a lot of money. A visit to the local library costs nothing extra. Low-cost opportunities for teaching and entertaining young children abound. You do not have to buy expensive toys. When my older daughter was three, her favorite Christmas present was the large box in which our new dishwasher was packaged. That box became her house; her E.T. doll was her husband. In our first home, the box took up a lot of the limited space available. I still remember the tears that flowed when we finally put "her home" in the trash. Our girls loved playing in my old two-person pup tent. All children need is an opportunity to let their imaginations go. That does not happen when they are watching television. **Kids should learn to entertain themselves.**

Your kids also need plenty of play time with other kids. It is up to the parents to provide these learning experiences. Parents must consistently look for ways to encourage their children to interact with other children. Many neighborhoods and apartment complexes have an abundance of kids. Maybe there are cousins close by.

I remember one thing my wife missed most about not working outside the home was contact with other adults. Anyone would probably need a break from being around small children all day, every day. She became part of a group with four other friends who called themselves Mother's Day Out. One day a week, one mother would take care of the children for a few hours while the other moms went out. For one out of every five sessions, she was the babysitter. For the other four days, she had some free time with adult conversation and moral support concerning parenting. The other positive outcome was another opportunity for the kids to progress with their ongoing process of socialization.

During the formative years, parents must supervise their children's media exposure. Computer use needs to be monitored carefully. Young children are not emotionally ready to handle the things they will see in 'PG' and 'R' rated movies. Here is an example. My family laughs about this incident today, but when it happened, it was not the least bit funny. To make matters worse, the whole thing was my fault.

A movie I had seen as a kid, "The Swamp Thing," was coming on TV and I wanted to watch it. Sarah, who was three or four years old at the time, wanted to watch it with me. The movie was filmed in black and white and was mildly frightening by today's standards. I patiently explained to Sarah that the monster was just a man in a rubber suit wearing a mask. The whole movie was just pretend. I asked her if she understood what I was saying. Her eyes grew wider and wider as she quickly answered yes.

My wife was in the next room listening to this conversation. She walked into the room and said, "Jack, this is not a good idea. You will be the one getting up in the middle of the night, not me." My brilliant response was, "But Sarah knows this is all pretend. Right, Sarah?" Her eyes were as big as silver dollars by now as she replied, "Yes, Daddy."

We sat down and watched the same movie I had seen as a boy. I had forgotten that I was then 13 or 14 years old, not three or four. Whenever the creature appeared, I reassured my daughter it was all pretend. She told me she understood but snuggled closer and closer each time the monster emerged from the murky water. When the movie was over, everything seemed fine. We enjoyed our dinner and put the kids to bed without any problems.

About two o'clock in the morning, we were awakened by hysterical screaming from the girls' room. Sarah was yelling something about a Swamp Thing in her closet. I could barely make out through horrified cries that a monster was trying to get her. I felt an elbow jab firmly into my ribs. This was my cue to get up and save my daughter from the awful creature. To add to the chaos, the baby woke up. Betsy was crying at the top of her lungs. Oh, the humanity! It took half an hour to get them calmed down. When I asked Sarah if she remembered anything about make believe, masks, and rubber suits, she started crying again. I think I would have preferred tangling with the Swamp Thing instead of my wife's elbow for the rest of the night. I learned my lesson.

I share this example because it leads to a more serious point I want to impress on young parents. This was just a minor incident. There was no long-term emotional damage from "The Swamp Thing," but let me give you another example which was also the parents' fault. Our girls had been at their friends' house and returned home with some news that concerned us. They told us they had been watching 'R' rated movies. Betsy and Sarah were four and seven years old at the time. The parents were not paying attention or did not care enough to monitor what the children were watching on cable television. From this point on, when our kids wanted to play with these children, my wife would tactfully arrange it so they would come over to our house.

The children from this family experienced excessive problems in middle school and high school. As young adults they are still trying to recover from the rough start to their lives. We cannot say for sure how many of these problems stem from seeing too much too soon. It is up to the parents to censor inappropriate media influences when kids are young. If the parents fail at this important task, their children's emotions will not develop properly.

Young children do not have the emotional maturity to process violence and sex. When they do observe these activities, their developing emotions will be damaged. They become desensitized to violence. They have trouble separating reality from what they see on TV and computers. In short, this exposure can cause serious problems in the coming years. **It is the parents' job to protect the innocence of childhood.**

Parenting forces us to learn how to compromise more than ever before. This is not as easy as it may sound. Parents have to think of the baby's needs before their own. I was 28 years old when I became a father and I was used to controlling my spare time. When our first daughter was born, my life changed drastically. I thought I knew what was coming my way, but with hindsight, I can tell you that until I had my own children, I had no idea. I never fully appreciated my own parents until I became a parent myself. My wife insisted I do my fair share of changing diapers, giving baths, and feeding the baby. I confess I would have been happy to let her do all those things.

A rude awakening greeted me each evening when I arrived home. On the drive home from work, I would be thinking: I am so tired; it will be great to come home and relax, eat a good meal, read the paper, watch a little TV, and go to bed. At about 5:30 to 6 o'clock, my wife's thinking was more along these lines: Jack should be home soon; this has been a long day and I need some help. He can take care of the baby while I finish preparing dinner; he can change the next dirty diaper; he can give the baby a bath while I clean up the dinner dishes; he can put on her pajamas and get her ready for bed. Babies get tired and cranky at the end of the day, too. I learned quickly that for a parent of young children, arriving home from a long day at work did not mean it was time to relax.

I eventually became used to the new routine. An important benefit was derived from all the baths, diaper changes, and feedings. It made my relationship with our daughters much closer from the beginning. Again, I have my wife to thank for this. I would not have done any of those things if she had given me a choice. How many fathers today start out the formative years as a supportive partner doing their fair share? This direct involvement is important. Raising little children is hard work, and the primary caregiver needs help.

Parents get one chance at the formative years. If you invest your time, love, and energy during the first six years, you will likely have fewer problems as your children grow. If it is not your spouse or you providing this vital influence, who is it to be? That choice will be one of the most important decisions you ever make as a parent. Samuel Palmer once gave the following advice to parents: "Begin to instruct as soon as the child has any notion of the difference between good and evil. And this is as soon as he or she knows your smile from your frown."

Busy parents need to slow down so they have the **time and energy** for their children's formative years. These are special times that in hindsight will pass quickly. One day you are bringing your newborn baby home from the hospital and it seems like the next day he or she is boarding the school bus for first grade. Frank Bogan wrote an article published in our newspaper titled "Grief and Loneliness Line a Father's Empty Nest." He had taken his youngest child to college and was home reminiscing. He wrote:

> "And so I lean against the wall and I fiddle with a plastic plaque. It bears a tiny handprint squished into it years ago at preschool...a favorite project of preschool teachers who smile wickedly as they send the things home to unsuspecting young parents. They know that some day you'll sit in an empty room and wrench your guts out over the little kid ghosts it stirs. Ghosts that whisper "Hi Daddy" so softly that only you can hear them."

Notes for Chapter One
The Formative Years

Notes for Chapter One
The Formative Years

The purpose of discipline is not to punish, but to correct.

Chapter Two
Discipline and Respect

Whatever method of discipline a parent chooses, it will be more effective if the children believe they are loved and respected and that the parent has their best interests at heart. Toddlers will not fully understand, but older children will be able to sense these feelings much sooner than some parents realize. Gentle words, hugs and kisses, good-natured smiles, and soft touches help establish these important bonds. Tell your children you love them every day. Is it not ironic that at times we treat our colleagues at work, or even complete strangers, better than we treat our own families? Why do we do it? I know I have made this mistake. My point is simple: if your child loves, trusts, and respects you, he or she will be easier to discipline. The bonds must be formed from the very beginning.

In this chapter I will discuss the following points:

- discipline helps children make positive decisions even when adults are not present
- the uniqueness of each child must be taken into account when selecting the most effective method of discipline for him or her
- spanking as a last resort and how it differs from child abuse
- the importance of unconditional love as it relates to separating the doer from the deed
- the connection between discipline and respect
- parents must work as a team in disciplining their children
- no must mean no
- consequences should be fair, and

- parents must strike a balance between being too strict and too lenient.

Children will grow up and have minds of their own. Parental control should not be your objective. What you want to instill in your son or daughter is child-control, to be in charge of his or her own desires, actions, and habits. The key is to teach them to make good decisions because they know it is the right thing to do, not because some adult is watching them. When kids lack self-discipline, they will be more likely to make poor decisions when an adult is not present. If you can develop a relationship with your children where **they believe one of the worst things they could do is disappoint you,** you will be on the right path.

Each child's personality is unique. Our daughters' personalities are similar in some ways but different in others. I have identical twin nephews and the same holds true for them. As a parent, you must figure out what form of discipline works best for each child. Many children will respond if you just sit down and talk to them. You can explain what they did wrong, reassure them of your love, and the problem is often solved. Some will even react positively to a change in your tone of voice or look of disapproval. Other children will correct their behavior after a period in the time-out chair or having privileges and material possessions removed for a time. One of my childhood friends grew up in a home where the parents did not believe in spanking their children. They were a quiet, gentle family, and all three kids have grown into successful adults. They were never spanked. Not once.

Unfortunately, there are a number of children who are stubborn and must learn things the hard way. For these challenging individuals, spanking can be effective and fear can be a good motivator. After you have talked to these children, have put them in time-out, taken away privileges, and given them another chance, it is time to get their attention with something they will understand: PAIN.

Although suffering a spanking is not a fond memory, our girls still smile and shake their heads at the mention of the words "wooden spoon." We were getting ready to go somewhere and Betsy, four years old at the time, did not want to get dressed in the clothes that were appropriate for the occasion. After a lively discussion, Betsy threw a classic temper tantrum. We did not want to be late, so, after several minutes, my wife reappeared in Betsy's room with the dreaded wooden spoon. After a couple of swats, our uncooperative daughter put on her clothes and reluctantly joined us in the car. On occasion, our older daughter also experienced the sting of the swat. Thereafter, most negative behavior ceased if my wife or I asked, "Do I have to get the wooden spoon?"

Spanking a young child should only be used as a last resort, when all else has failed. Many adults do not understand the difference between spanking and physical abuse. A spanking should never be carried out in anger or without explaining to the child what it was he or she did wrong. It should never be carried out with enough force to cause injury. On the other hand, to be effective, spanking must cause some discomfort. After the spanking is over, reassure with loving words but make it clear that you will not tolerate repeated inappropriate behavior. This reassurance is separating the doer from the deed and is important because your children must know your love for them is unconditional. After the spanking, you may have a child who is briefly angry and resentful, but one who will get over it. If the spanking is handled in the proper way, in most cases your child will rarely, if ever, repeat the troublesome behavior.

The basic purpose of discipline is not to punish, but to correct unacceptable behavior. For kids with the type of personality that responds most effectively to physical consequences, it must always be in the back of their minds that it could happen again. If children get out of line and see the parents give looks of disapproval or notice changes in their tone of voice, the children need to realize that if their actions continue, a spanking will follow. The memory must be painful enough to put some fear into the child. The lingering fear helps to develop the self-discipline required to curb the negative behavior.

For generations, parents have said, "This is going to hurt me more than it will hurt you." Spankings are unpleasant for both parent and child, but the parent's role is to set limits and, when the limits are exceeded, impose consequences. Undisciplined children create problems for schools, law enforcement agencies, neighborhoods, and ultimately themselves. They will be unable to build a happy and productive life. If parents fail to instill self-discipline, children cannot be expected to succeed. **Parents who raise undisciplined children are parents guilty of child abuse.**

The concepts of discipline and respect are linked together. Think of your best teachers, coaches, bosses, or other esteemed leaders in your life; I have no doubt their ability to create a disciplined environment was one of the reasons you respected them. Most people want structure in their lives. Things run more efficiently, people treat each other better, and individuals know what to expect. Without discipline as an important part of its foundation, a family, school, business, or any other organization will most likely fail.

I had a young man in one of my classes who was disruptive and disrespectful. As his teacher, I tried to help this troubled student achieve some level of success. Several talks with him, his parents, the counselor, and the dean, failed to correct his negative behavior. I had to ask how much longer I could allow one student to disrupt the entire class? If I had him removed, would I somehow be failing him as his teacher? Could I have done more to try and help him?

At the high school teaching level, most of us usually end up following the wisdom of the farmer and refuse to allow one rotten apple to spoil the whole barrel. When the young man was removed from my roster, several students actually came up and thanked me. They told me their assigned seats were close to his desk in a different class the previous semester and, "he had ruined the class." The majority of kids sincerely want discipline and structure; as adults, it is our responsibility to provide it for them.

Young people's respect for authority figures has declined, whether those adults are teachers, school principals, law enforcement officers, business men or women, or even judges. A growing number of kids show little respect for **adults who place expectations on them followed by accountability.** Kids who do not respect their parents and siblings are more likely to be disrespectful of others. Nevertheless, their biggest problems will be self-inflicted. Success will be difficult to achieve for these young people with negative attitudes.

Effective discipline for children demands that the mother and father stick together. It is a mistake to have one parent take the side of the child against the other parent. This will cause emotions to run high and create feelings of uncertainty. In the end, the arguments will strain the marriage and add more stress to the life of the child. Differences of opinion are going to occur just as they will in any other aspect of family life. When this happens, the parents should discuss their differences behind closed doors. They must reach a compromise and present a united front to their children.

I remember a student whose parents openly disagreed on how they should handle their daughter's poor choices. As time passed, the young lady failed academically, abused drugs, was expelled from school, and ended up in trouble with the law. For this middle class family, figuring out how to pay for the services of a lawyer in addition to a psychotherapist added fuel to the fire. As the parents tried to deal with these problems, the disagreements continued. The resultant stress caused marital problems. The family was beginning to tear apart. I believe most of the problems could have been prevented if the mother and father had worked as a team and supported each other regarding the discipline of their daughter.

If parents do not support each other, another problem can develop. When children want something they will ask one parent. If that parent says no, they will then ask the other parent. The second parent may not be aware that the first parent has already said no. This is like starting the clock on a time bomb. It will blow up sooner or later. **Parents must work as a team.** As Abraham Lincoln once said, "A house divided against itself cannot stand."

If parents expect to be effective disciplinarians, they must start in the formative years. More and more young parents accept or rationalize inappropriate behavior in their young children. I wish I could make them understand Shakespeare's Julius Caesar, who said, "Cowards die many times before their deaths, the valiant never taste of death but once." Parents must be valiant and have the courage to do what must be done, to deal with each situation as it arises. **When two- or three- year-olds do not respect adults, their behavior will only deteriorate as they grow older.**

I was once in a grocery store and observed a young child who already exhibited little respect for her parent. She took things off the shelf and told her mother to put them in the grocery cart. Her mother would calmly return the items to the shelf and warn the child not to do it again. The little girl went down the next aisle and repeated her actions. The mother warned her again. This continued up and down the aisles. Eventually, the little girl threw a temper tantrum in front of the customers and workers. The embarrassed mother gave in and purchased the things her daughter wanted.

When this three-year-old is 13, her parents will still be embarrassed as well as frustrated, angry, and disappointed. They will have themselves to blame. My experience tells me that parents like the mother in the grocery store are quick to **blame the schools when their children fail.** I once asked such a parent a question he was unable to answer. I had his 16-year-old daughter in class and she was a constant problem. Her father blamed me for much of his child's failure. This girl was having trouble with other classes, too. The counselor had informed me her record indicated a consistent pattern of disciplinary issues throughout her school experience. Insubordination, lack of respect, disruptive behavior, excessive absences, being late to class, sleeping in class, and not completing homework were typical notations. After a long and frustrating discussion with the girl's father, my question was: "For one semester, I teach your child in my class for fifty minutes a day. How do you expect me to successfully correct her behavior when you haven't been able to in sixteen years?"

In my career as a teacher, I have seen many such sad examples. I have witnessed students delivering profanity-laced tirades right in front of their parents. They show no respect whatsoever. I have felt sorry for these couples as they sat there, embarrassed and humiliated. I have seen ugly shouting episodes and heard students scream "shut up!" to their parents. Personally, I have been cussed out by students on more than one occasion. **This lack of respect results from a lack of discipline.**

These same parents cannot get their children to follow their own family rules and policies. They cannot trust their kids. They have confessed to me that they do not know what to do. From their viewpoint, they have tried everything and nothing seems to work. You can give many of these teenagers the best advice in the world, but they probably will not follow it. It is frustrating for these parents when they come to understand there is no simple solution to their dilemma. **Serious discipline problems that have been years in the making are not solved overnight.**

As parents, we all make mistakes. My hope is you will not make any *big* mistakes. I heard a mother say, "I was too nice to my kids when they were young. I acted more like their friend than their parent. If I could do it over, I would be a lot tougher on them." That mother's regret conveys good advice for young parents. The kids in her family experienced problems with drugs, academics, sexual promiscuity, and generally negative behavior. This lady and her husband have been through hell for failing to do what was required from the beginning. **You are not your child's friend; you are the parent.** While this does not mean you cannot be a friendly parent, kids will not always understand or agree with your decisions and rules. Do not give in! They will figure things out as they get older and wiser. At times your kids will test your patience with the persistent question: WHY? While it is preferable to explain why you want them to do something, you do not always owe them an explanation. This is especially true when they would not comprehend it anyway. Nothing is wrong with ending these exchanges with a firm, "Because I say so."

Do not threaten or give a warning to your child unless you intend to act on it. Be proactive. Anticipate problems before they occur and be ready to respond. To return to the example of the mother and daughter in the grocery store, there is nothing wrong with your little angel picking out *one* small treat. All children are going to want candy, breakfast cereals, cookies, and soft drinks when they see them lined up before their eyes. Those items tempt many adults, too. They are particularly hard to resist as you go through the check out lines where the grocer has strategically placed yet another candy display. I have seen some impressive temper tantrums at that very spot.

Kids are smart. If the parent is unsure or inconsistent, their children will sense the insecurity. You are the boss and there can only be one of those. Allow your children one choice of a treat. If they start asking for another, tell them no. If they ask again, you have a number of options: you need to select the one that works best for each child. You could put the first item back on the shelf and inform them they now get nothing this time. A disapproving look or change in your tone of voice may work if your child knows from experience that if they do not back off, a spanking may be the result. This is not brain surgery. **Respect must be earned and it comes as a byproduct of effective discipline.**

Consistency is vital. It does not take long for a young child to figure out that **no means no!** A teacher in our school has a sign in her room which asks, "What part of the word **NO** don't you understand?" This is a problem for a growing number of students who have not yet learned to accept no for an answer. Unfortunately, I see some parents who do not understand that no means no, either. At our commencement ceremony, parents were directed not to get close to their son or daughter receiving their diploma and take a flash picture. A professional photographer was hired for this purpose and parents could order a picture from the photographer. A restraining cord was set up to keep the people back from the stage. I was assigned to keep watch in this area and it was irritating to see how many parents tried to shove past me. I had to call security to assist me with one of the more aggressive fathers. **Parents cannot expect kids to follow their advice and ignore their example.**

Parents should not send mixed messages. Do not give a warning unless you intend to act on it. It is vital for you to carry out the punishment you decide on. You need to apply discipline firmly and reasonably; try not to let anger throw you off balance.

I know of a parent who had a curfew for his teenager. One night, the boy came home forty-five minutes late. The parent was angry and when the young man finally walked in the door, his father was there waiting for him. The heated conversation ended when the father grounded the boy from going out with his friends for the next three weeks. After a week and a half, the father gave in to his son's complaining and let him go out with his friends. This parent made several common mistakes. First, the punishment was too severe for a first time infraction. It is likely his anger affected his judgment. We can all remember saying and doing things while angry which we regretted later. Second, he did not follow through with what he said the punishment would be. If repeated over time, **kids start to realize "no" in fact means "maybe."**

Some students try to apply this same way of thinking at school. When they break one of my class rules, they seem surprised and angry that I impose the consequence I said I would. Policies do not mean much to these kids because in their experience **adults have not consistently held them accountable for their poor decisions.** Eventually, these kids meet with much tougher consequences. The prisons are full of people who did not think they had to follow the rules and laws. The father should have explained to his son how worried he gets when his son is late. Parents envision all types of horrible things happening to their kids as they are waiting for the door to open and see their children safely home. He might have asked his son to call home and explain his tardiness. As long as this does not happen often, most parents will give their child a few minutes leeway.

Another important aspect of discipline is **maintaining a balance between being too strict and too lenient.** Most kids have a sense of fairness and justice. When parents are too strict, children may rebel. As these young adults start college, they experiment with new boundaries. For the first time in their lives these freshmen are away from their overly strict parents and many rebel to the point where they do not make it through the first year. **For other hard line parents, they will experience the frustrations of dealing with rebellious children way before the college years arrive.**

In conclusion, I would summarize my philosophy on discipline and respect with the following points:

- Your children must love and trust you. They must believe you have their best interests at heart.
- Each child's personality is unique. You must figure out what method of discipline works best with each child.
- Spanking and child abuse are *not* synonymous.
- Separate the doer from the deed. When disciplining children, do not make it a personal attack. Kids must believe their parents' love for them is unconditional.
- Kids need discipline. If parents do not instill discipline, their children will have trouble succeeding in life.
- Parents should work as a team regarding the discipline of their children. They must present a united approach and when disagreements occur, compromises must be worked out in private.
- You need to begin applying effective methods of discipline in the formative years.

- No must mean no. Be consistent. Do not give a warning unless you intend to act on it.
- You are not your children's friend, you are their parent.
- The punishment for a poor decision should be fair. Strive to attain a balance between being too strict and too lenient.
- Children will most likely be disrespectful to parents who are ineffective disciplinarians. This lack of respect can contribute to a breakdown in the parent-child relationship.

Notes for Chapter Two
Discipline and Respect

Model a strong work ethic. Make your expectations clear and see to it that your children live up to them.

Chapter Three
Chores and High Expectations

Years ago, a neighbor asked me how I managed to get our two daughters to work with me in the yard all afternoon. I winked at my girls and responded, "We don't feed them until they complete their work – no work, no food." I smiled at my two daughters who were both giggling. I remember thinking it must be frustrating for parents who cannot get their own children to help with the unending chores that go along with home ownership.

In this chapter I will discuss the following points:

- children should help with household chores starting with putting away their toys at the conclusion of play time
- assigned daily chores must be appropriate for the age level of each child
- as children grow, jobs to be completed once a week should be added to chores done on a daily basis
- there is a connection between household chores and successful students
- helping the family fosters feelings of pride, importance, and teamwork, and
- learning to like what you do, not do what you like.

I have always maintained that young children can do much more than many adults believe. This is especially true when it comes to helping out around the home. If a toddler can pull a toy off of the shelf to play with it, then that same child can certainly be taught to put it back on the shelf. If you want your kids to help, you have to break them in at a very young age. Some psychologists would call this technique conditioning. To begin with, the parent must work with the toddler to pick things up when playtime is over. Children must be shown *how* to put things away. Some parents have permanent play areas for their kids and just shut the door when they do not want to look at the toys scattered everywhere. Parents with larger homes have the luxury of playrooms, but most young parents start out in smaller homes with limited space. In either situation, children should be taught to put things away when they are finished with them. The goal is to condition them from the beginning to help out.

One potential problem is that it is quicker for parents to pick up the toys. Parents who do not want the hassle of dealing with a reluctant toddler take the easy way out by doing it themselves. This approach can become a pattern that will contribute toward the development of the proverbial "spoiled brat." If you invest the time, love, and energy when your children are young, you will reap the rewards of a teenager you can be proud of, and one whose company you truly enjoy. I recently overheard my wife tell our daughters, "Not only do I love you, but you have each grown into someone I would choose for a friend." I thought this was a nice compliment to our girls and an indirect statement of pride in herself as their mother.

When young children learn what you expect, then you start helping them do it on their own. This will not happen overnight. Our kids were no different from other children. They did not want to put their toys away. As a parent, it is pointless to spank or yell at your children consistently to get them to do what you expect. However, if your children will not do as you ask at the age of two, they almost certainly will not do as they are directed when they are older.

One idea is to make a work chart for each child. Adjust the expectations according to the child's age. The charts could look something like this:

BETSY'S CHART (three years old)						
CHORES	MON	TUES	WED	THURS	FRI	SAT
Brushed Teeth						
Picked Up Toys						
Picked Up Room						
Got Dressed						
Made Bed						

SARAH'S CHART (six years old)						
CHORES	MON	TUES	WED	THURS	FRI	SAT
Set Supper Table						
Food/Water for Dog						
Picked Up / Toys-Room						
Laid Out Clothes						
Made Bed						

My wife made up these charts and posted them on the refrigerator. Each night our family would sit down together and see how the girls did that day. We had little stars we could stick in each box for the day and chore. We would tell them how proud we were and how much we appreciated their help. We explained when they got a star in every box we would give them a reward at the end of the week. There are all types of little surprises you can give them. We used to go to the Dairy Queen or allow them to choose an inexpensive toy. Use your imagination.

It is important parents do not perform tasks for their children if they can do them on their own. Basketball coach John Wooden was quoted as saying, "Why can't we realize that it only weakens those we want to help when we do things for them that they should do for themselves?" As usual, Coach Wooden had the right idea. Using these charts has another benefit. It is also a practical way for you to introduce to the child the concept of the calendar. You can begin teaching about days, weeks, months, and years.

Once our kids fell into the routine of doing what we expected them to do, the charts were no longer necessary. As they grew older, we explained to them that **each member of our family had an important role.** We all had chores to do. The rewards were no longer given out each week. I wish I could tell you everything worked like clockwork, but that was not the case. There were still occasions when our girls procrastinated on putting their things away, but in general they improved steadily as they grew older.

Another effective method to get them to pick up their toys involved walking into their play area with a garbage bag and filling it up with anything not put away. When we did this, both girls were worthy of an Oscar for their performances. The tears and pleading were truly impressive. We would tie off the top of the bag, put it in the attic, and inform them they would get their toys back at some future time. We stuck to the time we set. I can tell you this approach worked well. Another benefit was they learned quickly that **just because they cried and whined, we would not change our minds.**

As our girls grew, we expected more from them. In addition to their daily chores, we added weekly duties. Whenever possible we tried to do this work on Saturday mornings. The kids surprisingly grew to enjoy this schedule. Our day would begin with a pancake breakfast. We would turn on the cartoons and they would help me with the cooking. It was not long before they wanted to make the pancake batter, pour it on the griddle, and flip them over by themselves. This was a good opportunity to teach them to follow instructions. We were also able to introduce the concept of fractions with ideas such as one-half cup of milk or making a recipe and a half because Grandpa was coming by to join us.

After breakfast, we would all work together. Everyone had an assignment. My job was sweeping and mopping the floors. My wife cleaned the bathrooms and washed all the towels and sheets. In addition to cleaning her own room, each girl was responsible for dusting and vacuuming one floor of the house. **We all worked together.** When our daughters were young they thought all children were doing the same thing. By the time they were older and learned otherwise, they were used to our routine and cooperated for the most part without complaining too much.

It was interesting to listen to our girls talk about other children. When we had families come over to visit we usually encouraged them to bring their kids. Some families would visit and we hardly saw the kids from the time they arrived. At the end of the evening, when it was time to go home, they were still going strong.

On the other hand, we had visits from families with uncooperative children who refused to leave their parents' side. The adults were usually upstairs in the living room or out on the porch. Within fifteen minutes, these kids would be sitting with the adults. Their parents would tell them to go down and play with the other kids. The children would whine and say something like, "There is nothing to do." or "I'm bored." In these situations I found it difficult to keep my mouth shut. I wanted to tell these children that only boring people get bored. I did not want to offend our guests, but I also did not want time with our friends spoiled by their children.

These same children made our kids angry. They were not fun playmates and they disappeared when it was time to pick up the messes they made. Their parents would ask them to pitch in with the other kids but they could not get them to do any work. After our guests left, as soon as the front door closed, our two daughters would vent their frustration. My wife and I would sit and listen. When they calmed down, we would ask them questions like, "Why do you think the Smith children are fun and help pick up all the toys?" or: "Why don't you enjoy playing with the Jones kids and why don't they help put things away?" Even when they are young, kids can be amazingly perceptive. Our girls already had the whole thing figured out. They would make comments like, "Her mother tells her to do something and she won't do it; His father just lets him get away with it; Their parents should make them do it." Or, "You would never let us get away with that." I am reminded of the old saying: "out of the mouths of babes." **I strongly believe in making expectations clear and then seeing to it that your children live up to them.**

Many benefits flow from expecting your children to help around the house. Psychologist Dr. John Rosemond published an excellent newspaper article titled, "Good School Work Starts at Home." He made the point that children should be assigned a fair share of day-to-day housework. He went on to say, "It makes sense, doesn't it, that a child who comes to school already accustomed to accepting adult assignments will have fewer problems accepting assignments from teachers? The more responsible a child is within his or her family, the more responsibility the child will demonstrate at school." The effect on children of parents who either do their chores for them or give in to their whining and complaining should be obvious. As a teacher, I have to deal with these irritating, unmotivated, and disrespectful children every day. To make the problem worse, most of their parents have expertly rationalized the situation.

Other benefits of parents working with their children as a team include a feeling of importance in the children. They are contributing to the overall good of the family. They are part of something special; their efforts are appreciated. One of the most basic emotional needs for any person of any age is to feel loved and appreciated. For young children, it is important to have this need fulfilled constantly.

Further, when your kids help with the household chores, they will be more careful about making a mess. When they know they will be the ones who clean it up, they will be more responsible. For example, one of my pet peeves was with some of the children who came to our house and, after playing outside in the spring or after it rained, kept their shoes on and tracked mud all over the house. If they had been required to clean up that mud, I have no doubt they would have taken off their shoes before coming inside.

When kids work hard, they learn to take pride in their home and respect the things it contains. They are more considerate of other peoples' homes when they visit. I used to cringe when some kids would lie down on our nice sofa and put their feet on it with their shoes on. These same types of kids damaged things whenever they came over. I also know that some of them met with a lot of difficulties when they reached middle school and high school. Common sense should tell any parent there is a definite connection.

Pride is another important segment of the child's personality that parents must teach. We are not helping our kids by letting them get away with doing the bare minimum or inferior work. When you inspect the chores they have completed, there are some old sayings you can apply when appropriate. These are some of my favorites:

- It is better to do a job right the first time than to have to explain why you did not.
- Pride is doing your very best, even when nobody is watching.

- A job poorly done stands as a witness against the person who did it.
- People will usually forget how fast you did a job. They will remember how well it was done.
- Be the labor great or small, do it well or not at all.

I was always using these old sayings with my kids. They would usually roll their eyes and say something like, "Where do you come up with this corny stuff?" I did not care. I have recited them ever since I began teaching and coaching. I can tell you that even though kids act as though they are not listening, they mostly are. Many children enjoy imitating their parents, teachers, and coaches. As soon as they realize you have a sense of humor, some of them will not hesitate to repeat what you say and how you say it. There are times when kids at my school will notice another student doing something and use one of my sayings before I can even say it myself. We usually look at each other and laugh. I will add something like, "Great minds think alike."

At home, our kids have quoted their mother or me on things we do not remember saying. In my classes, I will occasionally start to say something and the students respond almost in unison, "Mr. Gangstad, you already told us that three or four weeks ago." Be careful what you say; they are listening more than most of us realize.

Most kids have to be taught how to work. This is another good reason to expect them to help out from the beginning. One of the biggest concerns I have for high school students today is a poor work ethic. Many will say, "If I don't want to do something, I'm not going to do it." Parents have let them get away with this negative attitude.

I called his home to speak with the parents of one failing student. I explained to his father that one of the main reasons his son was not succeeding was his refusal to do any homework. We had my student pick up on a second telephone and the three of us discussed the problem. I asked the young man why he was not doing his homework. He answered, "I don't want to. I don't like it and I'm tired of doing all this stuff." I asked him to hang up so I could talk with his father. The father then told me his son was having the same problem in other classes. He also confided that he could not get him to help out around the house. If his son did not want to do something, he did not do it. **Parents must not tolerate this behavior in their children.** I suggested that if there was not an immediate attitude adjustment, the father should start taking away his privileges. He should make up any failed courses during summer school. Poor decisions must result in negative consequences, otherwise learning will not occur.

Most of us have to do more things on a daily basis that we *do not* enjoy than things we *do* like. Kids better learn this early or they will be in for a tough transition when school starts. When children need to expend effort to achieve a goal, the reward of accomplishment is much more satisfying. Without exertion and sacrifice, it is easier to accept defeat and failure because they have not worked hard enough to expect success. When they invest their time and effort, they probably will not allow mistakes and disappointments to stop them. As Og Mandino said, "Failure will not overwhelm you if your determination to succeed is strong enough."

As our kids grew older, Saturday morning chores became a thing of the past. Parties, soccer games, and other activities made this old routine impractical. Parents must be flexible in their expectations. I learned it was not a good idea to expect them to do their chores as soon as they arrived home from a slumber party. I grew to dread those two words - SLUMBER PARTY. They would stay up most of the night, arrive home in a terrible mood, and sleep all afternoon. So we adapted. We told them they must get their jobs completed before they went to bed on Sunday night. For the most part, both girls cooperated. The goal was completion of their chores. Unless there is a good reason, why make them do it right away?

As adults, I hope our daughters know how to take care of themselves. We have tried to teach them to be independent. I expect them to be hard workers. I want them to understand that in life **it is better to like what you do than to do what you like.** One of the best things parents can teach their children is how to get along without them. Parents should not pave the road for their children. Their responsibility is to give them a road map. In the proper measures, hard work and struggles are necessary to prepare children for the real world.

I will close this chapter with the following story that helps make my point. A boy found a butterfly cocoon which soon developed a small opening. He sat and waited for a long time as the emerging butterfly struggled to force its body through the little hole. It seemed to stop making any progress, having pushed itself out as far as it could. So, the boy decided to help the butterfly. He took a pair of scissors and snipped off the remaining bit of the cocoon. The butterfly emerged easily, but it had a swollen body and small, shriveled wings. The boy continued to watch the butterfly because he expected that at any moment the wings would enlarge and expand to support the body which would get smaller. Neither happened. In fact, the butterfly spent the rest of its short life crawling around with a swollen body and shriveled wings. It was never able to fly. The well-intentioned boy did not understand that the restricting cocoon and the struggle required to get through the tiny opening were nature's way of forcing fluid from the body of the butterfly into its wings so it would be ready for flight once it achieved its freedom.

Notes for Chapter Three
Chores and High Expectations

The decisions you make will determine the quality of your life.

Chapter Four
Decision-Making and Mistakes

Values are the most significant factor in a person's ability to make decisions. Positive values are as important to children as a compass is to the captain of a ship. They point the way. Many decisions become easier to make when one is sure of his or her values. One of the assignments I have given a class I teach is to write a response to the following question: How much influence does the media (television, music, movies, internet, magazines, newspaper, etc.) have on the decision-making process of today's teenagers? I also direct them to list what they feel are their family's top five values at the bottom of the page.

When they have completed their written work we have a class discussion. It is interesting to hear what my students have to say. Some kids say the media has a significant influence. Others express the view that the media has minimal influence on teenagers' decisions. In their words, "Kids do what they want to do." I interject several points that seem to question their statements. For example:

- After the Columbine tragedy, some sources were blaming the actions of the two teenage murderers on the influence of violent video games and the music of Marilyn Manson.
- There was an incident where two brothers, aged three and five, set fire to their home which burned to the ground. The parents blamed the fire on *Beavis and Butthead*. The boys had watched an episode where the animated characters started a fire when they were playing with matches.
- There is a scene in a movie in which young people lie down on the center-line of a highway for the thrill of cars and trucks

speeding past their bodies. After the movie had been out for a few weeks, the movie company considered cutting this scene from the film because so many teenagers were doing it in real life. At least one person was run over and killed.

- An older child killed a younger child while performing a move he saw on a televised professional wrestling match. Other young people are getting seriously injured while imitating these moves in their back yards. Some of the kids are even filming these dangerous acts with their personal camcorders.

I ask them if they know why I had them list their family's top five values at the bottom of the page. What is the connection between family values and the influence of the media on kids? If children grow up in homes where adults model the positive values they are teaching their kids, the influence of the media will most likely have minimal effect. Those who grow up in this kind of environment can listen to a song with violent or profane lyrics and enjoy it, unaffected by the harsh sentiments because they simply like the sound of the music. They can watch violent movies or play sadistic video games and **they understand it is entertainment.** The values their parents have taught them are what prevent these children from becoming involved in the negative influences they see and hear in the media. Like many people from my era, I loved *The Three Stooges.* I laughed when the Stooges hit, poked, and gouged each other. However, I knew if I poked my little brother in the eyes as Mo did to Curly and Larry, I would be severely punished. It was always clear to me from a very young age that these programs were only for entertainment.

When kids grow up in homes where positive values are *not* taught and modeled by adults, the influence of the media can become a significant factor. **Negative values result in negative decisions.** Not only will counterproductive programs in the media have a negative effect, so will other detrimental influences including peer pressure. When children develop a pattern of poor decision-making, they dig themselves into a hole so deep it becomes difficult for them to climb out. I have seen this happen too many times.

In this chapter I will discuss the following points:

- values and self-esteem are important factors in decision-making
- parents must teach their children how to make positive decisions
- five suggestions to guide the decision-making process
- bad decisions must result in negative consequences
- problems created by over-protective parents
- turning a mistake into a positive experience
- learning from the mistakes of others, and
- the connection between positive decision-making and eating dinner together as a family.

Some parents are not certain what to do about all the negative influences their children are confronted with on a regular basis. It is much harder to be a kid today than it was when I was growing up. Adults have always teased younger generations about how much tougher it was in their day. As soon as an adult starts out with, "Hey, when I was a kid..." a teenager will usually cut them off saying something like, "Yeah, yeah, you had to walk five miles to school every day through snowdrifts, uphill both ways." The kids will roll their eyes and tune out the adult.

Most parents acknowledge what today's kids are up against. The question is how to protect and guide them. The most effective step parents can take to counteract the negative influences in modern society is teaching their children to make good decisions. **Successful**

decision-making is learned: we are not born with this ability. In some cases I think it is a mistake for parents to try and isolate their kids from reality, building a protective bubble to shield them from all the terrible things that happen out there in "the jungle." Their hearts are in the right place, but unfortunately, this approach may not help their kids in the long run.

Parents make the choices for their children when they are small. As the pre-school years come to an end, children must begin making more of their own decisions. As they start this important process, their parents will still need to guide them. As children grow, more situations will arise where Mom and Dad will not be there to tell them what to do. Parents must prepare their children for these times. I have some suggestions we used with our kids, which were helpful. Use your own judgment to determine at what age your children can comprehend and apply these concepts to their lives.

When your children ask themselves if they are making the right decision, the solution can usually be found by answering these specific questions.

1. **What are all my options? Who do I trust to give me good advice?**

Encourage your children to seek out the suggestions of someone who has been there and done that. This person may be the parent, a grandparent, sibling, or someone in the community. I am always willing to help students who come to me seeking advice. I find it one of the most satisfying parts of my profession. Teachers, coaches, and counselors are good sources of knowledge and experience. Kids need to realize there are choices available they may never have thought of on their own. They need to understand that help is there, and that they should take advantage of it. All they need to do is ask.

2. **Will I think well of myself when I look back at what I have done? Would I want family and friends to know about my choices?**

"If my parents find out about this they will kill me!" Most of us can remember saying something similar to this during our childhood. In my case, there were times I went right ahead and did the deed anyway. Sometimes I got caught and sometimes I got away with it. Back then we were sneaking out at night, throwing snowballs at cars, or viewing *Playboy* magazines at a friend's house. More temptations combined with an increase in poor decision-making skills have raised the stakes for today's adolescents. Should I get into the car when I know the driver has been drinking alcohol? Should I go to that party when I know there's a good chance for trouble? Should I have sex? Should I experiment with drugs? Should I steal a drive in my parents' car even though I do not yet have my license? Should I shoplift? The need to use good judgment is consequently more important than ever before. **Decisions made with the hope that nobody will find out are usually wrong.**

Some former students invited me to a class reunion. As I was leaving, a former student approached my wife and me to say goodbye. He said, "I want to thank you for something I learned from you that has kept me out of more trouble than I can remember. You taught us about decision-making. One of your questions was would you want family and friends to know of your decision? That advice has helped me more than you will ever know." Brian took out his wallet and showed me a picture of his two children. He continued, "When my kids are old enough to understand, I'm going to teach them the same thing." It is the parents' responsibility to teach their kids how to make good decisions. Parents should be their child's most important teachers.

3. **Does the choice I prefer seem sensible to me? Never mind what my friends say or think; what do I think?**

We hear a lot about peer pressure today. How influential is it? For many young people, it is a powerful factor. For others, peer pressure will have little influence on their behavior. Why is there such a difference? The answer is self-esteem. When a child has high self-esteem, peer pressure will not have as much influence. For kids with low self-esteem, it can be a significant problem.

Let me cite an example. Two teenage girls have boyfriends. They have been dating these boys steadily for over six months. Both girls think they might be in love. The boyfriends have started pressuring the girls to have oral sex and intercourse. The girls are not sure what to do. Sex is exciting and tempting, but they do not want to risk getting pregnant or possibly contract a sexually transmitted disease. They are concerned about losing their virginity. The girls worry how their parents would react if they found out. Eventually, the boys feel they have been patient long enough. Each one has reassured his girlfriend he loves her, and goes on to say, "If you truly love me, you will give yourself to me and do as I ask. There are plenty of other girls willing to have sex if you won't. If you refuse, I'm moving on."

The girl with low self-esteem will go through a decision-making process like this. "I think I love this boy. I really don't want to have sex with him yet, but I don't want to risk losing him. If I say no to his demands and he leaves me, I may not be able to find another boyfriend. I won't be happy without him in my life." The girl gives in and has sex with her boyfriend. All too often, it is sex without contraceptives.

The girl with high self-esteem thinks more along these lines. "Honestly, I'm not ready for sex yet. If I get pregnant, I may not be able to achieve the goals I've set for myself. My parents and other family members would have a difficult time dealing with this situation. If my boyfriend truly loved me, he wouldn't keep asking me to do something I don't want to do. If I tell him no, and he leaves me for another girl, he never loved me in the first place. It will hurt and I will miss him, but sooner or later I'll meet someone else and move on with my life." This girl says no and forces her boyfriend to make a decision. She will be able to handle it either way.

Self-esteem or the lack thereof goes a long way in determining how well a child deals with peer pressure. I have observed several warning signs of low self-esteem as follows. Children with low self-esteem frequently:

- will refuse to try something because they are afraid they might fail
- become negative in their outlook on just about every aspect of their lives
- enjoy making fun of others
- always want to be the center of attention, or they become very shy
- become apathetic about things that should be important to them: school/grades, appearance, and taking good care of their bodies (sleep, nutrition, and exercise)
- do not feel they are as good as other kids
- believe nobody likes them
- worry excessively about what other people think of them
- are sexually promiscuous
- are overly concerned about their appearance (hair, make-up, & clothes) and
- abuse alcohol and other drugs.

As I observe the decision-making process of kids, the two factors that appear to be **the most important influences are positive values**

and high self-esteem. If a parent can instill those two qualities in their children and teach them to seek out the answers to the five questions written in bold print, their kids will make good decisions. Of course, they will still make mistakes, but they will most likely avoid the big mistakes— those with long-term consequences.

4. **Can I live with what will happen as a result of my decision? Will I feel guilty?**

A person can do something in an instant that he or she will regret for a lifetime. A few years ago, I was on a ladder in our front yard cutting a dead limb out of a large oak tree. I wanted to mow the yard after I finished pruning the trees. I figured if I pushed myself, I could complete all my chores and be able to play golf the next day. I was in a hurry and I became careless. I lost my balance and fell off the ladder. When I hit the ground, I heard the bones in my lower legs snap. X-rays confirmed both legs were broken, the left worse than the right. The orthopedic surgeon had to operate and put some screws into my lower tibia. The cartilage throughout the ankle joint was damaged. As I lay in the hospital ER contemplating this turn of events, I said to myself, "If I could only have five seconds to do over again, I wouldn't be here with two broken legs. I wouldn't have to spend the whole summer flat on my back or in a wheelchair. I wouldn't have to go through the rest of my life limping around on a damaged left leg. If I could just have five seconds to do it over, I wouldn't be in this situation."

After we make a bad decision we frequently do not get a second chance. We must deal with the consequences. I am willing to bet there are many people who would wish to have five seconds of their lives to do over. As bad as my judgment on that occasion seems to me, it does not come close to some of the negative decisions made by students in my school.

Students of mine have been killed or seriously injured in car accidents as a result of carelessness and alcohol use. Others have been shot because they were in the wrong place at the wrong time. Students have been jailed for the rest of their lives for murder. Some of my students have committed suicide. Some were high on drugs when they did so. I have seen students experience emotional problems after an abortion that did not seem wrong at the time they had it. I have watched student athletes throw away promising careers because they chose to get involved with drugs. I have felt sorry for pregnant girls as they try to make it through my class without vomiting from morning sickness and I have witnessed others struggle to manage their lives as both teen mother and full time student. Many of these young women dropped out and did not return.

If teachers at most high schools in the country were asked to tell stories of poor student decisions, they would probably come up with a list similar to mine. Whenever possible, share examples of bad choices with your own children and follow up with a discussion. I call this planting a seed. It will not always appear to make an immediate difference, but it might help them in the future. A wise person learns from the mistakes of others. Ordinary people learn from their own mistakes. A fool never learns.

5. **How will this decision affect me? Will anyone be hurt? What will be the likely outcome?**

Parents need to teach their kids to be proactive. I have heard pregnant teenagers say they wish they had remained abstinent. After students have been expelled for possession or tested positive for drugs, some state they wish they had never become involved with drugs. When athletes have been declared academically ineligible, they admit they should have studied from the very beginning. Unfortunately, this insight arrived too late.

It is easy to see what you should have done once the consequences of the bad decision are known. The key is to anticipate these consequences beforehand. This practical skill will be invaluable. How do you teach this to kids? One of the best ways is to let them make mistakes when they are young so they can learn from them. I heard four common sayings growing up that help make my point.

1. You made your bed, now lie in it.
2. You are going to have to learn this the hard way.
3. Give them enough rope to hang themselves.
4. You will stew in your own juices.

Make sure your children experience the negative consequences of their bad decisions. That experience is an important step in the learning process for positive decision-making.

Some parents overly protect their children instead of teaching them that in real life a person must learn and overcome. It does not mean you are a bad parent when your child makes a poor choice. We all make mistakes. Contentment does not come from the absence of problems but through the ability to deal with them and cope. Happiness and success are byproducts of effective life adjustments. When children succeed on their own merits, they will have a better chance of achieving true happiness.

We had an athlete transfer to us from a nearby school. Rick had been getting in trouble for years and his parents wanted him to make a fresh start. When it came to sports, this young man was the type of player all coaches would want on their teams. His difficulties were away from the athletic field. The boy's father was a nice man who obviously loved his son. However, whenever his boy made a mistake, he would cover for his son. He never held Rick accountable for his actions.

When he forgot something at home, Rick would call his dad who immediately brought the item to school. When he started getting in trouble with teachers and administrators, the father took his son's side. When he was involved with some vandalism, the father paid for the damages and his son paid nothing. When Rick was close to being declared academically ineligible, his father was on the phone pleading with teachers to give his son a break. I saw this man at our high school at least once a week.

At the end of Rick's senior football season, his father approached several football coaches and said, "I want to thank you for everything you have done for my son. I have been worried about him for years and I didn't know if he would ever graduate from high school. Through your influence, I believe you have literally saved his life." As he walked away, I shook my head and told my coaching partners, "He still doesn't understand. Rick will be going off to college next year but he hasn't learned to stand on his own two feet."

The young man was talented enough to earn an athletic scholarship. He had to attend a junior college in another state because his grades were not high enough for him to be admitted to any of our state and private universities. His father would not be there to cover for him anymore. He flunked out in his first year and took a job back in his hometown. Rick was arrested a few months later for dealing drugs, and the last I heard he was still in prison. I am hopeful some jail time will teach him what his father never did.

Mistakes are part of life. The goal is to keep them to a minimum, and through good decisions avoid the serious errors in judgment that have long-term consequences. As a parent, you must also teach your kids how to handle mistakes, turning them into a positive experience. How? Try getting them to follow this simple three-step process.

1. Admit it. 2. Learn from it. 3. Don't repeat it.

Be honest with your children from the beginning. Do not rationalize poor choices. During the formative years, the mistakes will be small. Deal with each one openly and honestly.

I remember when our daughter was three years old and we went to visit some friends who had an eight-year-old daughter. This girl had a doll our daughter wanted. When we returned home, we noticed our little angel had an unfamiliar doll in her possession. We saw this as a chance to teach an important lesson so we sat her down and had a discussion about stealing. We then drove back to our friends' house and had our daughter return the doll and apologize. I believe when you consistently take care of little problems, the big ones may never happen.

After your child has admitted an error of judgment, it will be important he or she learns from it. This will be a time when your child must feel secure in the belief that your love for him or her is unconditional. Make sure there is an appropriate consequence, but remember to separate the doer from the deed and do not make it personal. Look on such an event as **an opportunity for your child to grow and become a better person.**

I am convinced that families who do not sit down and eat dinner together miss out on several teaching opportunities. When our kids were young, we ate dinner as a family almost every night. Occasionally, my wife and I would discuss the poor choices made by students at our schools. We would ask our girls to express their thoughts on these stories. The discussions were objective and yet thought-provoking. They provided a forum for proactive decision-making by our kids. Sometimes we mentioned alternative solutions to consider. The girls began to express themselves with growing confidence. They realized their thoughts and feelings were important. We encouraged them to think by always asking them to justify their opinions.

I hear some parents say they cannot get their children to talk. If parents keep the lines of communication open, ask the right questions, and truly listen, most kids will talk. Once our children started, I had to get used to "Dad, you're interrupting me." Some nights, I had trouble getting a single word into the conversation.

Parents need to make family dinners more important. Certainly people are busy, but **the way in which they spend their time is a reflection of their priorities.** According to one study by The American Psychological Association, for adolescents the dinner table serves as an informal forum. Children can talk about problems and dilemmas. It also gives them a time to talk about their accomplishments. For the family as a whole, meals together help keep the lines of communication open and make it easier for parents to give advice, as well as offer an opportunity to teach proper manners.

A study by Thomas S. Weisner, Professor of Psychiatry at U.C.L.A., found that meals serve purposes in addition to eating food. Families were asked what was important to them about mealtime, and they ranked conversation and sharing of information ahead of eating. At the dinner table, people decipher things that happened during the day. They are telling the result of a prior plan which leads to future events. Problem-solving and planning are closely related activities. A report published in *The Journal of the American Medical Association* found that, "Teenagers who have dinners together with their families are less likely to engage in risky health behaviors. Examples of these risks are ones that result in emotional distress, violence, suicidal thinking, and substance abuse. **If there is a strong parental connectedness that demonstrates warmth, love, and caring, the kids make better decisions and fewer mistakes."**

After your children have admitted their mistakes and learned from them, we get to the most important benefit of this process. They will most likely not repeat them. Experience to a large extent comprises mistakes you will not repeat. I have heard it said that the difficulties we face in life should make us better, not bitter. If parents do not hold their kids accountable for their own actions, they cannot grow as people. The decisions they make will determine the quality of their lives.

Notes for Chapter Four
Decision-Making and Mistakes

Love your children for who they are, not what you want them to be.

Chapter Five
Self-Esteem

Parents can do much to nurture self-esteem in their children. Of all the ideas I will share with you, the most important for children is the need to live in a loving and stable home. When children have a solid family supporting them, everything else is more likely to fall into place. To achieve this goal parents must set an example and make their family a top priority. A supportive family will multiply your happiness and divide your sorrow. It will be a genuine source of inner strength upon which a child can draw over and over during the tough times he or she will inevitably face. Even under ideal circumstances, it is not easy being a kid. For children growing up in homes with serious problems, it can be even more difficult to attain high self-esteem.

Selecting the person we will marry could be the most important decision any of us ever make. One out of two marriages ends in divorce. Nearly one out of three children born today is illegitimate. Parents raising kids following a divorce or those without a legal partner are more likely to have additional issues that can hamper the children's development of self-esteem. Families who do not fit the traditional mold should take heart from the message at the end of a movie titled *Mrs. Doubtfire*. Robin Williams is dressed up as a kind, funny, and wise elderly woman who has her own children's television show. A young girl has written a letter to Mrs. Doubtfire who reads it on her program. After reading the letter, she responds to her young viewer.

> "There are all sorts of different families, Katie. Some families have one Mommy. Some families have one

> Daddy or two families and some children live with their uncle or aunt. And some live with their grandparents or some children live with foster parents. And some live in separate homes, in separate neighborhoods, in different parts of the country. And they may not see each other for days, weeks, months, or even years at a time. But if there is love, Dear, those are the ties that bind and you have a family in your heart forever."

No matter what the circumstances, kids need to feel part of a family. In this day and age, the word family can have many meanings, but they all have *love* as a common denominator.

In this chapter I will discuss the following points:

- the importance of a loving and stable home
- positive eavesdropping
- family videos and photographs
- the danger of comparing siblings in an effort to motivate
- memory boxes, baby books, and birthday parties
- frame an award and hang it on the child's bedroom wall
- the influence of people outside the family circle
- love your children for who they are, not what you want them to be
- appearance
- eating habits, and
- progressing from unconditional praise during the formative years to complimenting children only when they truly deserve it.

People must be able to love and respect themselves before they can love and respect others. That is what self-esteem is all about. Being part of a quality family is a good start, but parents can initiate other actions to facilitate the development of self-worth. Next time you are at a park, playground, or swimming pool, listen to the small children who have a parent present. You will hear them shouting out things like, "Watch me, Mommy, watch me." Wise parents will give their young children plenty of praise and encouragement. They need this love and attention.

I recommend a technique I call **positive eavesdropping.** If children are in another room and hear their parents talking about them, they will listen. This is another opportunity to praise your children. When you are talking with your spouse, tell him or her some of the good things that happened during the day. An example might be, "Betsy said the entire alphabet today all by herself. I'm so proud of her." When a child overhears that sort of comment day after day, it will have an enormous influence on his or her self-esteem.

You can also do this when you are talking on the phone to the grandparents. They love to hear good things about their grandkids so it is a win-win situation at both ends of the line. An example might be, "Sarah said the funniest thing after her first day of kindergarten. She had never seen identical twins and there was a pair in her class. When I asked how her day went she told me there were two boys in her class and they both had the same head." Laugh together when your children say something funny. Have a good sense of humor. Do not take yourself too seriously and have some fun with your kids. I remember reading a poem titled *Children Learn What They Live.* The poet wrote that if children live with tolerance, encouragement, praise, fairness, security, acceptance, and approval they will learn to like themselves and find love in the world. This is good advice for all parents.

Kids like to see themselves on television. Every family needs at least one "shutter bug" to record the special moments. Not only will this help your kids but the videos will be a keepsake you will treasure in the years to come. Record your kids making funny faces, counting to ten, saying the alphabet, dancing, saying nursery rhymes, singing songs, and showing off their Halloween costumes. Have your children explain a project they are working on and ask them questions about it. One way to organize the videos is to number them and insert note cards explaining what is on each one. The card could look something like this one:

	FAMILY TAPE #7 - MAY 1985 TO OCTOBER 1986
05/07/85	The new trundle bed
06/07/85	Sarah's piano recital
07/28/85	Running through the sprinkler
08/05/85	Sarah explaining her library project "Diarama"
10/31/85	Halloween - Indian Princess and Raggedy Ann
12/14/85	Betsy explaining her Sunday School project - The Manger
12/22/85	Santa's visit
12/25/85	Family Christmas
2/6/86	Sarah and Betsy making funny faces
2/15/86	Sarah's sixth birthday party
3/7/86	Betsy's third birthday party
6/21/86	Sarah - Sleeping Beauty / Betsy - Nursery Rhymes

This system not only keeps the videos organized but also makes it easy for your kids to pick out the ones they want to watch. When children view themselves, they will laugh at the funny things on the television. They will also see some of the smart and cute things they do. They will become more poised. They learn to express themselves assertively and become more articulate.

In addition to videos, taking photographs is also important. I prefer to organize these in photo albums and I think of them as our family yearbooks. With digital cameras, pictures can be saved on a computer and e-mailed to family and friends around the country. Whatever method you choose, make these photographs accessible to your kids. When you get a favorite, have a print made and frame it. Put the picture somewhere in the house where you and the kids will see it. These pictures will make you feel good when you look at them and provide another way to show your kids you think they are special. An additional benefit of these photographs and videos is they present the opportunity to teach your kids about different family relatives. At a young age, they can start learning about grandparents, grandchildren, aunts, uncles, nieces, nephews, and cousins. This process helps establish at a young age the importance of family.

Whenever your children earn a special honor or award and receive a certificate or picture, frame it. Hang it on a wall in their room and **let them pick the location.** This works well for honors such as athletic awards, championship team pictures, and academic recognition. Inexpensive frames are easy to find. As the years go by, more and more frames will go up. Every day they will see visible proof of their successes.

Be careful about comparing one child with another. Realistically, all parents do it to some extent. As long as this is done in private, it will not cause trouble. Avoid the following comparisons:

- Why don't you make good grades and be more responsible like your brother?

- You should get more involved at school and play sports like your sister.
- Why don't you get a part-time job and earn your own money like your brother does?
- Why can't you stay out of trouble and be as good as your sister?

When parents compare siblings, it can create several problems. First, Andy's resentment grows. He begins to doubt he will ever measure up to his brother or sister. The parents reinforce this feeling each time they make a disparaging comparison. As time passes, Andy begins to feel no matter what he does, it will not be good enough. His self-esteem continues to drop and he may even give up trying.

At my school, we had a young man on the football team who was ready to start his junior year. Jon was a gifted athlete, and we expected great things from him over the next two seasons. On the first day of practice, he was nowhere to be seen. The team was just as surprised as I was and could offer no explanation for his absence. That night I called him on the phone and we had a long conversation. Jon told me he did not think he wanted to play football anymore. When I asked him why, he explained that his older brother had just graduated from our high school in the spring. He was one of the best football and baseball players in the entire state and had been very popular with his teammates and classmates. He ended up being a top draft choice for a major league baseball team. For the past few years, Jon had been living in the long shadow cast by his successful older brother. He did not want to follow in his brother's huge footsteps. He was afraid of the mean comments he anticipated being directed toward him. Jon's self-esteem was very low.

I talked him into coming back on our team. I convinced him that the coaches did not expect him to fill his brother's shoes. We would not make the comparisons he feared. We only asked that he come back and give us his best effort. Jon returned but his confidence had been shaken and he was unusually nervous before our first game. We were opening the season against our biggest rival. They were ranked number one in the polls and were the defending state champions. There would be a big crowd at this game. Fortunately, the story has a happy ending. Jon played an outstanding game. He intercepted three passes and scored a touchdown. He was the key player in a huge victory. Jon went on to have two great seasons for our football team. He was All-State and set two records that stand today. Jon turned down scholarship offers because he decided on a career in the military. The last I heard he was still in the Marines and doing well.

There is an important message in this story. Do not compare a successful older sibling to a younger child in your effort to motivate him or her to improve. Treat each child as an individual. Encourage your kids to do their best. Help guide them into areas that highlight their strengths. Kids already compare themselves to others. Parents need to use their wisdom to minimize comparisons. The young man in this story was ready to give up football because his self-esteem was low. He was unable to see his untapped potential because he was focusing on negative thoughts. It is the parents' responsibility to support their children and build up their self-esteem, not break it down.

Comparing children with each other can have another negative consequence. It can cause tension in the sibling relationship. Parents can nurture this bond or help tear it apart. Constant comparisons will make it more difficult for the children to become close with each other.

Having a successful older brother or sister should be an asset. The positive influence of another good role model in the life of a child can be invaluable. Our older daughter received a special birthday present from her younger sister. She purchased a frame and had the words "Still Looking Up to You" engraved along the top. The framed picture was of Betsy looking up at Sarah when they were four and seven years old. As Sarah opened her gift, they hugged each other and shared a few tears. I know this may sound corny to some people, but this remains a favorite memory for me of my daughters.

Another suggestion is to start what I call a memory box. The concept is simple and you should begin as soon as possible. Get some type of container to save all the special keepsakes for your children. I think it works best when you make one for each child. We purchased some inexpensive plastic storage boxes. Each memory box could, for example, contain the following:

- cute childhood drawings
- photographs
- cards and letters with special messages written to your child
- awards— second place in spelling bee, third place on track & field day
- programs from plays, recitals, or athletic events.

Anything of sentimental value can be saved inside their memory boxes. Pictures or articles in the school or local paper could be included as well as letters announcing an honor they have earned. You will get into the habit of saying to yourself, "I'll just put that in her memory box." Every time they look through their mementos, it reinforces a feeling of importance and being loved.

Along these same lines, consider making a baby book for each child. New versions make this task easy and are available at card shops/stationery stores. They contain things like newborn footprints from the hospital, the birth announcement, the family tree, a written message from each parent for their child to read in the future, first words, a list of visitors and who brought gifts, humorous stories, and many other things you will be glad you compiled. Put these books where the kids can get them out whenever they want to reminisce. They will do this occasionally, and they love to read through a book you put together just for them.

It is a good idea to have a birthday party for each child starting from age one. If possible, take pictures and videos. These parties do not need to be big and expensive productions. Even when money is in short supply, with a little imagination, you can put on an enjoyable party. Little children do not care how much money it costs. Almost all children love pizza, cake, and ice cream. A party also gives you another opportunity to work on manners. "Please" and "thank you" need to be used over and over until they become habit. As children get older, they should write a short thank-you note to relatives and friends who took the time to get them a present. Children should be expected to do this for gifts throughout the year. **Good manners and an appreciation for the things people do for them are important components of a positive personality.**

For the most part, people will treat you the way you treat them. Make sure your children understand this concept. Raise your children with good manners and teach them to be polite. Imbed the Golden Rule into their personality so they will be thoughtful, considerate, and kind. Foster the development of a good sense of humor. Encourage them to be unselfish. Share these classic adages:

- Forget yourself for others and others will never forget you.
- Blessed is the person who can give without remembering and take without forgetting.
- People wrapped up in themselves make small bundles.
- Takers eat well. Givers sleep well.

- Take an interest in people and people will take an interest in you.
- One of the sanest and most generous joys in life comes from being happy over the good fortune of others.

When someone says something nice about your child, make a conscious effort to share these comments. For example: "I saw Mrs. Doe and she said she spoke with you the other day when you were playing with her neighbor's daughter. She told me you seemed like such a nice girl and that you were very polite." Positive comments from people outside the family circle can provide a helpful boost to the child's self-esteem.

The transition from elementary school to middle school can be a tough time for many kids and I believe it can be especially difficult for girls. When our daughters were going through this phase, I gathered a collection of my favorite food-for-thought articles, quotes, and poems I had saved over the years. I put them in a three-ring notebook and included a hand written letter. I repeated how much we love them and how proud we are to have them as our daughters. I also added some basic advice about life. I tried to express in words how I felt about each daughter. I believe the girls appreciated this gesture and I think they still have those notebooks today. Another possibility might be to purchase some type of motivational book and write a special message to your child inside the front cover.

Many years ago, I received a Father's Day gift from one of my daughters that made a big impression on me. Her gift was a small book called *Wisdom for Fathers*. Each little page has a sentence or two with some advice for Dads. The one that stood out for me was **love your children for who they are, not what you want them to be.** Some parents try to force their children into being something they themselves desire and overlook what the child wants. Maybe your kids will take an interest in the things you want and maybe not. If they do not, it is important for you to support the things that hold their interest.

As your children get older, how you deal with their appearance will be another factor that affects their self-esteem. You and your child will be working against a culture that sends the message that appearance, sexuality, and popularity are more important than attitude and integrity. Teach your children that their appearance is important, but their character and personality are the top priority.

Be careful how you handle the issues of food and body weight. If you make too big a deal over it, the child may begin to think he or she is unattractive. Negative comments from kids at school are tough enough on their self-image. If children experience at home what they perceive to be more criticism, the results can be serious. One possible consequence of over-emphasis on weight and eating habits is the development of eating disorders. I have seen first hand how some of my students suffered as they were trying to overcome Anorexia Nervosa or Bulimia.

Trying to get your kids to develop healthy eating habits can be frustrating. Poor nutrition, sleep deprivation, and drug abuse are serious problems confronting education. At the high school level, not enough kids get up in time to eat a good breakfast. They stay up too late and want to sleep until the last possible minute. They skip breakfast and eat a lunch that typically includes a carbonated beverage, pizza, French fries, and pastries. These same kids eat candy and consume soft drinks for their snacks. They regularly follow this up with dinner at a fast food restaurant. These eating patterns, coupled with a lack of exercise, contribute to a growing problem with young people today: obesity. **Kids who are overweight are more likely to have low self-esteem.**

So what should parents do? They should make nutritious food available and set a good example. When you notice your kids are not eating properly, take a low-key approach. Explain what they should be eating, tell them why, and then drop it. The harder you push, the less likely it is you will achieve the results you seek. I remember how frustrated I would get when our own two daughters would not eat some of the meals we prepared. I recall thinking, "Here I am a health and PE teacher, and I can't even get my own two children to eat what's best for their overall nutrition." The sad fact is they were eating much better than many of the students in my school. As difficult as it was for me, I tried to be quiet, continue to make nutritious food available, and set a good example. Eventually their eating habits improved.

Consistently emphasize character and personality over appearance. Girls need fathers who model good behavior including the proper way to treat women. The same can be said for boys as they observe how their mother relates to their father. One of the best gifts a father can bestow on his children is to love their mother. Males will either love and respect females or use and abuse them. Girls and women with high self-esteem will be more likely to avoid abusive relationships.

I do not want to convey that appearance is not important. It should be something your child takes seriously. A person with an attractive appearance will have an advantage over those who are unattractive, but guide children to keep this concept in proper perspective. An attractive appearance will not guarantee a strong self-concept, although it will surely help. We do a lesson on appearance in one of my classes and discuss several topics related to this issue. I tell my students the old saying that God must have loved the average person because he made so many of them. Most of us are not born with the natural beauty and cosmetic enhancements of models and movie stars. However, if individuals take advantage of those aspects of their appearance they can control, they can usually still be attractive people. I follow this up by having the students make a list of all the things relative to appearance they can control. I rule out plastic surgery for this part. The kids do a good job and come up with a lengthy list. The students agree that one of the most important items on this list is a good body.

I used to teach an elective weight training class at our high school. Several years ago, a sophomore who resembled the classic "ninety-eight pound weakling" signed up for this class. Bill was an introvert and would only speak if I spoke to him first. He never smiled and did not appear to have any friends. I noticed that Bill worked hard every day and did all of the routines exactly as I directed. About ten weeks into the class, I saw him checking out his reflection in the mirror. His shirt was off and he was turning from side to side as he flexed his arms. Bill did not notice me as I walked through on my locker room supervision. The next time we were in the weight room, I walked up to him and said, "Your hard work is paying off. Look at the muscle on those arms. You're beginning to look like the Arm and Hammer Baking Soda box." I saw Bill smile for the first time. I continued with the compliments for the rest of the semester. I was pleased to see he had signed up to take the class for second semester. By the end of the school year, there was a positive change in this young man. Bill was talking to some of the other students, he smiled occasionally and had put on ten pounds of muscle.

I encouraged Bill to keep working out over the summer and recommended the YMCA across the street from our campus. He not only joined the "Y" for the summer but enrolled in my class for both semesters his junior year. By the end of his second year in weight training, Bill seemed like a different person. The scrawny introvert was long gone and in his place was a physically fit, happy, confident, and outgoing teenager. He was a leader in his class and a positive influence on the rookies struggling with getting into shape. He started dating and seemed to genuinely enjoy high school. I am convinced this transformation was due to the basic change in his lifestyle. Bill felt good about his own appearance and the way he was perceived by others. When a person sincerely believes he or she is attractive, it strengthens his or her self-esteem. As we know, this is important to kids at all grade levels.

Adjust your expectations as your kids grow up. When your children are in their formative years, they will need a consistent stream of praise and attention. Whatever they draw, paint, or make for you, tell them you love it. **As they get older, slowly begin to back away from unconditional praise.** You should not relate to an eight-year-old in the same way you do to a three-year-old. You need to progress to a point where you praise your children only when they have earned it. If what they have done is mediocre, do not tell them they did a great job. When parents make this mistake, it can have two negative consequences. First, kids will develop a false sense of security which may lead to a rude awakening when a teacher gives them a more objective and realistic evaluation of their work. Second, parents will lose credibility in the eyes of their child. Your compliments may not mean much to them anymore.

I had a student whose parents praised everything their son did. I was not impressed with the young man, but I could see he had potential. Greg would not listen when I gave him instructions. His effort on homework was unacceptable, and he was rude to his classmates. His test and quiz scores were low and remained at or below a passing level. He consistently told anyone who would listen how great he was at whatever was being discussed. His parents thought he should be every teacher's ideal student. After one frustrating day of class, I told him he probably did not need to come to school anymore because he already knew everything. He looked at me and said, "You're always picking on me. Get off my back and leave me alone. You never say anything positive to me."

I am a stubborn person. Occasionally, I wear students like this down. Fortunately, this young man started to conduct himself more appropriately. His grades began to improve. He started treating his classmates better. I began to take away some of his false confidence. I finally saw something I could truthfully compliment him on so I called him to my desk. He walked up to me with an expression that looked as though he thought he was in trouble again. I told him he was doing better and I was pleased with his progress. I did this in a voice loud enough for the rest of the class to hear. He actually smiled and thanked me. As he continued to improve, my compliments increased and he ended up passing the class. Unfortunately, for each student I am able to help like this one, there are too many who do not make it. Parents must support their children. However, only give them compliments when they have truly earned them.

It is up to parents to create a stable and loving home for the entire family. On the wall in my mother's kitchen is a framed paragraph titled *What Is a Home?* The author included some of the following qualities: warmth of loving hearts, first school and church for young ones, loyalty, comradeship, where children learn right from wrong, where joy is shared and sorrow eased, where children are wanted, and where money is not as important as loving kindness. Every child deserves to grow up in a home like this one.

Notes for Chapter Five
Self-esteem

Notes for Chapter Five
Self-esteem

The direction in which education starts a man will determine his future life.

~ Plato

Chapter Six
How to Raise a Successful Student

Education is a controversial topic today. You hear about it from the politicians and you read about it on the editorial page of the newspaper. Every election year education seems to resurface as a major campaign issue. Why? One reason is the number of young people who are not succeeding in our public schools. Citizens see how much of the taxpayers' money is allocated to education, and they are not satisfied with the results. Politicians respond to voter concerns by passing new laws and policies. I will make some suggestions that will help parents raise children who develop into successful students. **Implementing these ideas will, I am sure, be more effective than waiting for the government to do what parents should be doing in the first place.**

In this chapter I will discuss the following topics:

- teaching children to be self-motivated as opposed to parent-motivated
- the connection between parental interest and student achievement
- why parents must be enthusiastic toward their children's education
- a realistic approach to grades and report cards
- being a supportive, but not overly involved parent
- parents who live vicariously through the accomplishments of their children
- when parents volunteer, they should do so for the benefit of all the children, not to promote their own child
- communication with the teacher when problems arise

- celebrating academic excellence
- the development of mental toughness
- parents and teachers working together when disciplinary problems occur, and
- student excuses.

Children need to understand it is their life they are dealing with; they are not going to school to make good grades for their parents. Kids must learn to take a personal interest in their own education. When children understand this, **they become self-motivated instead of parent-motivated.** This insight makes a significant difference in the way a child looks at school and the importance of a good education.

At one point in middle school, our daughter set a goal to make "straight A's" on her next report card. She reached this decision all on her own. When she came home with her report card, I could tell she was not happy. I saw disappointment in her eyes as she handed me her report card. As I looked it over, my reaction was just the opposite. I was impressed. I said, "Sarah, this is an excellent report card. Great job." All her grades were A's except for one solitary B. Her comment was, "I got a B, Dad. Look at that one B." I replied, "But look at all those A's. Don't worry about the B. Did you do your best in that class?" She assured me she had done her best. I asked, "Is there anything you would have done differently if you had the chance to do it over again?" She shook her head. I concluded, "If you gave it your best shot, who can ask for more? Ten years from now, that one single B won't make any difference at all. What will make a difference is developing a good attitude and making an honest effort in whatever you do. If you accomplish this, you'll be a success and that's more important than any grade on your report card." This is what I mean by being self-motivated as opposed to parent-motivated.

Once you have taught your kids to take personal interest in their own education, it is important to help them keep school in proper perspective.

Two basic concepts help form the foundation of a successful student. First, parents must sincerely care about their child's education. It must be accorded a high priority within the family. The importance of this point is illustrated every September at my high school. Year after year I hear teachers make the same comments about our Back-to-School Night. They tell me they rarely, if ever, see the parents these teachers really need to see. These are the parents of students who are experiencing academic and/or behavioral problems. Their classrooms are filled with interested parents of successful students. **There is a definite link between parental interest and educational achievement.**

The second basic point is that **parents must be enthusiastic and actively involved with their children's education.** You need to do math flash cards, review spelling words, ask questions from study guides, proofread compositions, and listen to practice speeches over and over again. Many times you will arrive home exhausted from a tough day at work and this will be the last thing you want to do. It is at times like these that you need to show enthusiasm when your kids come to you for help. Remember the message from the Back-to-School Night experience: if Mom and Dad do not care, the children will not care.

It will take years before children develop a sense of ownership for their own education. The process begins as soon as the child's first activity is penciled in on the family calendar. Whatever the occasion, if possible, one or both of the parents should attend to support their child. The initial goal is to nurture the feeling that whatever your child is doing, it is important. Little League games, cherub choir performances, Back-to-School Nights, piano recitals, and even grade school carnivals are all events you should attend. It does not matter if it is the Cub Scout Pinewood Derby or induction into the local Brownie Troop, parents need to be there for their kids. If possible, grandparents and other relatives should go as well.

Back-to-School Night gives parents an excellent opportunity from the beginning to reinforce the importance of school. When you sit down at your child's little desk, do not count the minutes until you can return home. Instead, make the minutes count. Write a short note and put it inside the desk where your son or daughter will be sure to see it first thing in the morning. It could read something like this:

Hi Betsy:

I enjoyed seeing your room and sitting at your desk.
Your teacher seems very nice and said you were doing
a good job. I loved your drawing of the jack-o-lanterns
on the Halloween bulletin board. Mom and I love you
and are very proud of you. Keep up the good work.

Love, Dad

Your children will enjoy finding special notes written just for them. The next night at dinner talk to them about their teacher. Comment on their papers and paintings displayed on the classroom walls. Tell them about some of the parents you met. Explain how fortunate they are to be able to go to such a wonderful school. Your child will slowly but surely get the message that school is important and should be taken seriously.

When your kids are in elementary school, beginning with first grade, eat lunch at least once every school year with each child. Sit down at the cafeteria table with their classmates and enjoy the time with the little children. Remember to take your camera and get some pictures for the family scrapbook. When you sit down that evening to eat dinner together, tell your child how much you enjoyed sharing lunch. Pay compliments to their friends and ask questions about the ones you remember. Discuss anything funny that occurred. Laugh together and have fun with your kids. **Make them feel that what they are doing is important.** My wife volunteered to help the teachers chaperone class field trips. Her assistance was appreciated and allowed her to share the experience with our daughters.

I know it is difficult for parents to take time away from their jobs. Some will make the mistake of saying, "Maybe next week or next month." Those weeks and months will quickly turn into years. All too soon those parents will turn around only to see their kids have grown up. Many of us look back on our lives and say, "I can't believe how fast the time has passed." I doubt anyone on his or her deathbed would say, "I wish I'd spent more time at the office."

Be a supportive but not overly involved parent. Overly involved parents have their hearts in the right place; like most parents, they love their children and want them to succeed. In elementary school, these are the parents who eat lunch with their kids two or three times a week, not once a year. They constantly call the teacher about minor problems and overreact to create problems where none exist. **They do not allow their children to learn from mistakes because they quickly step in and cover for them.** Although these parents want to create a perfect world for their kids, they ultimately raise children who cannot cope with the everyday problems of the real world. These parents put too much time, energy, and focus on their child. The child's place in the family is out of balance. My wife says, "It's as if the child is under a magnifying glass in the hot sun. Through the heat of the parents' constant focus, the child's personality, perspective, and joy for life are burned up."

Other parents live vicariously through the accomplishments of their children. These adults use their child's success to feed their own egos. In their minds, they raised the child, so the credit for his or her success should go to them. They constantly talk about their own kids to anyone who will listen. They brag about them and enjoy comparing them with other children. Many were unable themselves to accomplish as a student or athlete what they expect their own children to achieve. The mother who never made cheerleader spends an inordinate amount of money and time for gymnastics lessons as her little girl is growing up. To give her daughter a better chance at being selected, she becomes friendly with the sponsor who picks the squad. When her daughter makes cheerleader, she acts like she made the cut herself. The youngster's cheerleading experience is spoiled by the mother's over-involvement.

This happens with fathers, too. The dad who never made the basketball team when he was in school overreacts when his son makes the team. He hangs around the team practice sessions. If his son does not get what he thinks is enough playing time, he is the one who demands an explanation from the coach. He signs his son up for camp after camp and puts too much pressure on his boy to improve his basketball skills. In the end, the experience is negative because the father will not allow his son to simply enjoy the game. I will discuss these situations in greater detail in the upcoming chapter on extra-curricular activities.

Many volunteer positions with which parents get involved have the potential for problems. Room mothers, PTO, Little League coaches, and Sunday School teachers are all examples of these voluntary organizations. **When parents choose to be a part of such a volunteer group, they need to do so for the benefit of all the children and not to promote their own child.** Some parents get involved in these positions to fight their child's battles in an effort to help them succeed. This can work at the lower levels, but in the middle school years the same child is often found to be inept at problem-solving and decision-making. When parents pull strings to advance their children to positions ahead of other kids, there can be negative consequences. First, the other kids will figure out and resent what is happening. This can cause problems in the child's relationship with his or her peers. Second, adolescents receive the message that they need their parents' influence and help to succeed. They begin to have trouble making it on their own. The negative effects of this approach will carry over into everyday school work.

Avoiding over-involvement can start with the parent staying out of minor neighborhood disagreements. When kids play together, occasional dissension occurs. Let the kids work it out. Conflict management and leadership skills start to develop when adults allow kids to settle disagreements by themselves. When troubles arise with other kids at school, communicate with the teacher only if the problem is ongoing. If an issue lasts more than a couple of weeks and is disrupting your child's ability to learn, get the teacher involved. If disputes develop between your child and the teacher, be a good listener. Make some suggestions and encourage your son or daughter to work things out with the teacher. Once again, if the problem is ongoing and affecting the learning process, then call the teacher and get involved.

Students today are under excessive pressure to make superior grades and anxiety levels can be high. This stress can originate from the student, the parents, or from a combination of the two. Much of the tension will be eliminated when parents take a realistic approach to grades.

With our own kids, we did not place an emphasis on grades. **We believed good grades to be a byproduct of effective study habits and consistently urged our kids to do their best.** That sounds simple, but there is usually a gap between what kids and adults think is an honest effort. In such cases, it is the parents' responsibility to make certain their kids truly are doing their best. It is your job to know whether your child is paying attention in class, doing all his or her homework on time, studying effectively for tests, attending help sessions where necessary, asking questions, and taking advantage of extra credit opportunities. When students do their best, assuming they have the ability, the grades will take care of themselves. On the other hand, if a child's best efforts result in an average grade, the parent should still give the child positive feedback.

Several benefits can occur from this decreased emphasis on grades. It eases part of the pressure when students are taking tests. A number of students go into tests with the mindset they must get an A on the exam or their parents will be upset. Various students are afraid they will have privileges taken away. Others worry that if they do not get an A on the test, they will not maintain or improve their class rank. **Grades become an obsession.**

With the philosophy I am recommending, students are more relaxed because they are confident in the knowledge they have done their best and that is what is expected of them. They think, "Whatever happens, I'll be able to live with the result, regardless of the grade. The most important point is to make an honest effort." There will still be some anxiety involved with taking tests, but it is all kept in the proper perspective.

I have known people who made excellent grades in school, but met with little success in the real world. Conversely, I have observed people who made mediocre grades and ended up very successful in life. Grades are important and should be taken seriously, but they are not the only barometer of an education. Once your child gets a job, his or her boss will not care about grade point averages, SAT scores, or class rank. The boss will value and reward dependability, positive results, work ethic, proper preparation, and the ability to get along with co-workers.

For our family, this approach to grades worked well. Even though the goal is to develop a sense of educational ownership, we all like to be acknowledged when we have done something well. Some parents reward their children with money. For example, a father will say, "I will give you five dollars for each A on your report card. For each B, you will receive two dollars." This approach works against the philosophy of self-motivation.

At the conclusion of each grading period, the local newspaper included an article listing the names of students who made the honor roll in middle school and high school. I would cut out the articles that included one of our girls and post it on the refrigerator. After a few weeks, I would take it down and put it in her memory box along with the report card. Occasionally, I would write a short note to congratulate them on their accomplishment. It would read something like this one.

Sarah:

Great job on your report card. We know you worked hard and your effort has paid off. Mom and I are very proud of you.

Love, Dad

This note only took a couple of minutes to write and the kids appreciated it each time they found one on their pillow or by their bathroom sink. Occasionally, the whole family would go to the local Dairy Queen after supper as a way of recognizing academic excellence. As the kids got older, sometime around eighth grade, they preferred to go out for dinner at their favorite restaurant instead of going to the DQ for ice cream. We were proud of them and wanted our kids to know it. (We could still stop for ice cream on our way home from dinner.)

Education majors are required to take psychology classes as part of their teacher training. In one of the classes I took, several psychological theories were presented concerning development of the personality. One of these theories, Abraham Maslow's Hierarchy of Needs, made more sense to me than some of the others. I appreciated its simplicity and wisdom. Maslow believed that human needs can be compared to a pyramid. His analogy is based on the premise that lower level needs must be met before higher level needs can be satisfied.

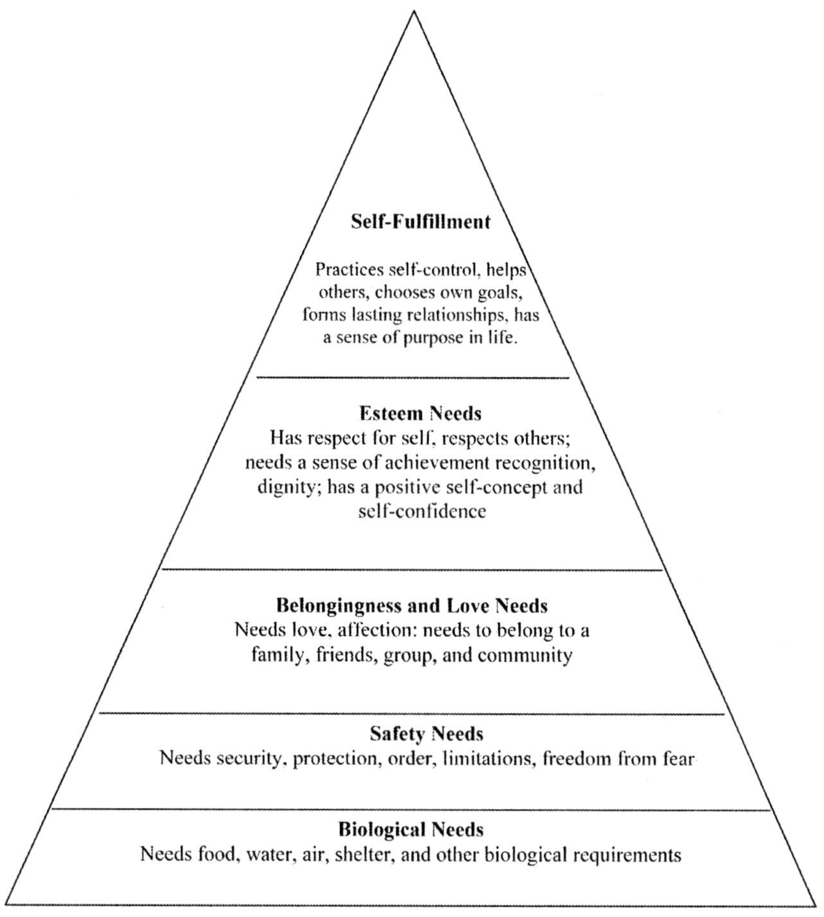

Maslow's Hierarchy of Needs

If you send a well-rested, well-nourished, and drug free student to school, your child will already be way ahead of many students before the first period bell rings. Your child will be able to listen to the teacher while others struggle to stay awake. Many students today will tell you school is boring. **I am convinced that what some of these kids perceive as boredom is really sleep deprivation, poor nutrition, and drug abuse.** Applying Maslow's Hierarchy of Needs, you can see that without adequate rest and nutrition, information being discussed in class becomes a secondary priority.

My mother used to tell my brothers, sisters, and me that if we were not vomiting, running a fever, or seeing a bone sticking out, we were going to school. Mom made certain all of us were well-rested and well-fed before going off to school each morning. My parents set a good example and practiced what they preached. We rarely saw our dad miss work. We rarely saw our mom stay in bed sick. They had made it through the Depression and World War II. My parents were mentally tough and passed some of that down to us. Once again, you cannot expect your children to follow your advice and ignore your example. You must model the behavior you expect from your kids.

Our school nurses are among the most patient, caring, and compassionate people I have ever known. Like most of us in education today, they have a tough job. I have always believed that many of students who visit the clinic are not sick. Our school nurses agreed with my observation. Why would students go to the health center if they are not sick? Do they want to skip a class? Are they just trying to take a nap? No. According to several of our veteran nurses, the underlying reason is that their own families do not care about them. Others have parents who are so busy or so overwhelmed with their personal problems, they cannot or will not be supportive.

The health center fills a void in the lives of these unfortunate students. Nobody at home shows them attention and compassion. They know our nurses will be the nurturing person absent in their lives. In one nurse's words, "It's like a little piece of home for these kids." All of us need to feel loved and appreciated. Parents must meet these basic emotional needs for their kids: failing to do so can have serious personal consequences, much less having a detrimental effect on school performance.

A girl was brought to our health center following a drug overdose during school. When our nurse called home to inform her mother, the woman's first response was, "Damn, I was just on my way out the door to play golf." The lady never even asked how her daughter was doing. Another nurse told me this sad story: A student received a ride to school from her mother who was on her way to work. Before leaving home and without the parent's knowledge, this girl took thirty sleeping pills. Upon arrival, the student went directly to the health center still wearing her coat and carrying her book bag. The girl said to our nurse, "I need to tell you something and I know you'll be mad at me." The nurse responded, "I'm not going to be mad at you. Tell me what's wrong." The girl admitted taking thirty sleeping pills. She was immediately transported to the hospital by paramedics to get her stomach pumped. She would confide in our school nurse, but would not talk to her own mother. How can a child be expected to be mentally tough when his or her basic emotional needs are not being met at home? It is surprising to me that these kids perform as well as they do because many find it difficult just getting by from day to day.

Parents make other mistakes which can hamper their ability to raise mentally tough children. Doug was a student in my third-period class and would arrive halfway through the period once or twice a week. School started at 7:30 a.m., but he would enter at about 9:45 or 10:00 o'clock. Doug always had an excused pass to admit him and the reason given was due to illness. He did not look sick to me, so after one of those excused tardies, I had a discussion with this student. Doug was not sick, but he was tired and he wanted to get some additional sleep. If he went to a concert on a school night, talked on the phone with his girlfriend until two o'clock in the morning, or stayed up most of the night playing video games and watching television, Doug did not think he should have to be at school for first period. He said he was so tired he really did feel sick when his parents tried to wake him. I told him I too was sick and tired. I was sick and tired of all his lame excuses. Children cannot make their dreams come true if they are allowed to keep hitting the snooze alarm. I already knew the answer to my question, but I asked Doug anyway: "How do you keep getting your pass marked 'excused'?" His mother would call in and lie to our attendance deans. If a parent calls in for a child, the attendance office will usually accept the story they are given. Not only do such parents raise kids lacking fortitude, they also teach their children to lie most convincingly.

Attendance is as important for school as in the business world. The whole process starts in kindergarten. A growing number of students do not have the structure and discipline in their lives to demonstrate dependability. Monday mornings are difficult for most of us, but when kids are worn out from the weekend, their parents do not help them by allowing them to stay home an extra day. It is also really irritating for teachers. Make-up work for absent students has become a problem at my high school. Whenever we give a quiz, or a test, or collect a homework assignment, an average class will have three or four students absent. In my high school, most teachers have five classes each day. Make-up work is part of a teacher's job and we understand it will always exist, but we do not appreciate it when the absences are not legitimate. Parents should make school attendance a priority for their children and set an example with their own work habits.

Parents who take their kids out of school to extend vacation time have also become commonplace in recent years. I understand there must be a few exceptions, but anyone who does this on a regular basis is setting a harmful precedent. They are usually trying to get a few extra days off or a better flight time at the airport. The rules apply to everyone else but them. These attitudes and practices send the wrong message to the student. The parents and students expect the teacher to provide all the make-up work and do not expect to receive a grade penalty. Attendance is such a problem for a nearby school district that they are in the process of adopting a much stricter policy regarding enforcement of school attendance. It is sad that some parents must be encouraged to insist their kids go to school. In my view, they need to wake up and get their priorities in order. Lack of dedication, lying, and selfishness are traits I see in an increasing number of kids today. Common sense tells us where they learn these vices.

For many years, my teaching schedule has been split between physical education in the morning and the classroom during the afternoon. As a PE teacher, I am worried about many problems I encounter on a regular basis. The kids I have been discussing, those who lack mental toughness, experience great difficulty when they are expected to change into a PE uniform and participate in activities involving physical effort. In the locker rooms, away from the direct supervision of a teacher, some of the more aggressive students refer to these children as wimps and tease them. No parent wants to see his or her child humiliated, but frequently these same parents not only helped create the situation, they also perpetuate it.

The overall fitness level of many young people has been declining at an alarming rate since I began teaching in the 1970s. Many factors contribute to this disturbing trend. For example, when kids complain about PE class, the parents are quick to write a note to excuse their children from doing any exercise. They will write that their child has a runny nose, sprained ankle, sore muscles, or other minor problems. Adults need to let their kids know that if they only work on the days when they feel like it, they will not accomplish much with their lives.

Just because kids do not feel 100 percent, does not mean they cannot go to school and participate in the activities.

Do not be an enabler for your child. Do not raise children who lack mental toughness. Almost all kids will gripe about getting up in the morning. Do not listen to these complaints— and set the tone from the beginning. As soon as you think your child can handle an alarm clock, buy one and expect him or her to use it. As kids get older, they need to develop the self-discipline to get up in the morning unassisted. I am frustrated by the number of times students have been absent from my class because their mother or father did not wake them on time and they consequently had no transportation to school. **Accountability for this issue should be placed on the teenager.** When the kids start complaining about a stomachache, headache, or cold, remember my mother's words. If they are not vomiting or running a fever, expect them to attend school. Most of the time, after a hot shower and a good breakfast, kids go to school, start talking with their friends, and feel better than anticipated. Children are capable of more than they think.

Another related problem is how changes in outside temperature affect some kids. They start whining about the temperature being too hot or too cold to go outside. It is almost a sure bet they have been allowed to get away with this behavior at home. Kids need to be outside so they can get some fresh air and exercise. Why do parents relent to this complaining? They simply do not want the hassle of dealing with a reluctant child and take the easy way out. Parents who consistently cave in whenever their children disagree with them end up with teenagers who do not respect them and who do whatever they please. Consistent giving in to complaints hurts children in the long run because it creates a lack of toughness that carries over to other aspects of their lives. Before long they use all these minor complaints as excuses for not getting the job done. Who can honestly write a recommendation for students such as these? Who wants to hire and promote such people?

Girls need to develop emotional strength as much as boys. When children are small, they occasionally fall down, getting bumps and bruises. There is a big difference between getting hurt and being injured. When young children are playing and receive minor hurts, do not overreact.

One summer evening, we attended a party which included several families. The adults were on the patio and the kids were playing in the back yard. A small child was running around and accidentally ran into another child. I saw the whole incident and the youngster just had the wind knocked out of him. The father was socializing with the other guests and the little boy walked up to his dad. He was trying not to cry as he told his father what happened. The boy's dad looked him over and said, "You're fine; go play with the other kids." The little boy choked back his tears, walked into the yard, and within minutes was again laughing and playing with the other children.

As long as a small child is hurt, *not injured,* this parental approach is appropriate. If that had been my young daughter, I would have handled the situation in the same way. Do not raise kids to be picked on by other children for their inability to handle bumps, bruises, or a runny nose. The mental toughness this father had started to instill in his son will carry over to school. When kids are small, they do not understand what you are trying to accomplish. As they grow older, they begin to notice weakness in other kids. You will hear your children say things like, "She is the biggest baby," or "All he does is whine and complain and his parents let him get away with it." Your kids will slowly begin to take pride in the fact they do not quit, whine, or complain whenever things get a little tough. They will be the ones who still get up in the morning when they really do not feel like it. They will not ask to miss school due to a minor headache, cold, or stomachache. They will not miss class by going to the school nurse when they are not truly sick. **Mentally tough students will excel while the others come up with one excuse after another.**

There are too many students who are inconsistent in their effort at school. They are fine for three or four weeks and then their performance drops off. They start taking three-day weekends on a regular basis. They sleep in and arrive at school late more frequently. Absences start to add up but are excused because a parent calls in to cover for the child. The excuses to rationalize these developing problems have been perfected. It is too bad because this approach will have a negative effect on school work and carry over into the work world. These youngsters grow into people who simply cannot be counted on.

If children get in trouble at school, they should be in even more trouble at home. When a disruptive child is causing problems, all a teacher should need to say is, "Do I have to call your parents?" This should be enough to get the child's attention and correct the inappropriate behavior. Unfortunately, more and more students today have parents who take their side against the teacher or just do not care. Kids who do not respect authority will have trouble succeeding at anything.

When I was in second grade, I was disrupting the class so the teacher had me come up to the blackboard. She drew a circle with chalk and I was directed to hold my nose against the board keeping it inside the circle. I was told to stand there until she told me it was okay to return to my desk. After a few minutes, I started feeling nauseated. No teacher wants a student to vomit in her classroom, so Mrs. McFadden immediately sent me to the school nurse. She called my mother who quickly came to school to take her sick boy home. Before we got in the car, I noticed Mom and my teacher having a short discussion. I began to feel even worse. On the way home, my mother informed me that if I had not been causing trouble, none of this would have happened. Mom shared my story with the entire family, all seven of us, at dinner that evening. In their version of tough love, I was raked over the coals. As soon as Mom finished, before I could say one word, my dad said, "Jack, you want to be the class clown. It seems to me you're more like the class jerk. We better not hear about this happening again." My supportive brother told me I was acting like an idiot. My loving sister said I got just what I deserved. They did not even ask for my side of the incident. I received the message loud and clear. I had better not disrupt my second grade class again, or else. I can assure you I did not want to experience the "or else." As I have noted, in the past, if teachers wanted to get a disruptive student's attention, all they usually had to ask was, "Do I have to call your parents?" Most homes I knew were like mine when it came to support for the teacher and school. In this respect, I think our daughters would tell you our home was similar to my childhood home. I believe this was one of the factors which helped them succeed as students.

On one occasion I was watching the local evening news on television when the top story involved a grade school teacher who had allegedly humiliated and abused one of her first grade students. The reporter on the scene said the child had been bound to her desk. Although the words were chosen carefully, the viewers were led to believe that rope and duct tape restrained this innocent child. The reporter interviewed the little girl's parents and lawyer who were commenting on how the teacher had damaged this student's self-esteem and caused her emotional pain and anguish. They announced that a lawsuit was being planned. The principal and superintendent were asked questions about the disciplinary action to be taken against this teacher. The reporter even asked about the possibility of firing this veteran educator. Too many members of the media relish covering negative stories involving schools. I have witnessed reporters and camera crews arriving at our school within minutes of a breaking story. I have been angered hearing the way the media twist words and blow things out of proportion and perspective. It is no wonder many people who work in the public eye have become suspicious and even hostile towards reporters.

To illustrate how some parents have changed, think back to my family's reaction when I had to hold my nose against the chalkboard. I had been a disruptive student and I needed to be taught a lesson. Along with the support of my family, the teacher sent a clear message that I had better shape up— and I did. When the entire story came out about the first grade girl, this is what actually happened. The little girl was continually getting out of her seat and disrupting the class. After several warnings, the child again left her seat. The teacher took a strip of Scotch Tape and attached one end to the side of her chair. She ran the piece of tape across the girl's lap, attached the end to the other side of her chair and informed the girl that if the tape came loose, she would be in more trouble. When the little girl told her parents what the teacher had done, they called their lawyer and went on the warpath. Is it any wonder so many young people do not have the proper respect for authority?

Teachers, counselors, and administrators care about children. We entered this profession because we enjoy being around kids. We find it rewarding to help them learn and grow into better people. Is every teacher so dedicated? No, but the majority of educators I observe have the students' best interests at heart. Unfortunately, a growing number of parents think the education system is out to get their child. Rather than collaborating with the teachers, they are quick to blame the school for their child's shortcomings. When kids have disciplinary trouble at school, they are unlikely to tell their parents the whole story. They do not necessarily lie, but through a process I call **selective amnesia,** they leave out key parts of the story in order to appear an innocent victim. It frustrates me as a teacher to see how many **gullible parents are quick to jump to the defense of their kids.**

On one occasion, an irate parent left me a profanity-laced voice mail message and wanted me to return her call immediately. Her son had been a disruption in my PE class for several weeks. I had sent him in to get dressed for causing problems and recorded the appropriate number of demerits in the grade book. In this particular incident, the young man had passed gas in front of the class during our flexibility routine. He innocently told his gullible mother this was a natural body function he was unable to prevent. This incident added sufficient demerits to cause the student's grade to be lowered. Since he was trying to maintain academic eligibility for athletics, both he and his mother were upset with me.

I called the mother during my prep period and we had an interesting conversation. When I explained the whole story, she actually apologized to me. The boy did not lie to his mother. He admitted he passed gas, but through selective amnesia, failed to mention a few other details. He did not tell her about the body language in his posture and forcing the release to be so loud it could be heard across the entire gym. He also left out the part about blaming it on the embarrassed girl behind him. He must have forgotten to mention shouting, "Did somebody step on a duck?" Of course, he was unable to see how my class was disrupted (and it did not settle down for five minutes) because he was in the locker room getting dressed. **When parents have a concern, they should contact the teacher first.** I have dealt with disappointed and embarrassed parents who felt the need to apologize after all the facts were explained. If parents are not satisfied after talking directly to the teacher, **then** they should go to the next administrative level for additional help.

Do not allow children to get away with making excuses. Parents who accept excuses raise children who substitute rationalization for performance. From the beginning, expect your children to complete the assigned job and take pride in that achievement. Lay this foundation early and it will carry over into their adult lives. If you fail at this important task, schoolwork will suffer. When they start school, encourage them to turn assignments in on time and to expect a grade penalty if they fail to meet the deadlines. If they miss a class or two for an appointment, get them back to school ASAP and do not allow them to take off the remainder of the school day. For the days your children are sick enough to miss school, advise them to see each teacher and make up work missed during their absence. Many schools have homework hotline telephone numbers for each teacher that can be used to keep pace with missed work.

One excuse I hear from students is, "I don't do well on tests." They go on to claim they know the material, but when they sit down to take the test, their mind goes blank. In my experience, the reason is they probably never knew the material. It is difficult to score well on a test when you have not prepared properly. Kids will not admit this because they want to take the easy way out and too many adults accept this excuse. One of the main problems in preparing for tests arises when students seek to memorize the material and quickly take the test before they forget what they just memorized. **There is a big difference between memorizing and understanding information.**

When students have a practical understanding of the material, they are more likely to remember it on test day. More importantly, they will retain the basic concepts after the class has been completed.

Students who just memorize facts without understanding the concepts being taught experience their biggest problem when they sit down to take the semester exams and unit tests. These are the tests that most affect their grade; they often provide the moment when their minds "go blank." For short quizzes, they may have been able to survive with passing grades. However, when held accountable for information covering ten chapters as opposed to one, they cannot remember the answers to all the questions. Since they never understood the main ideas the details confuse them. When students cannot apply facts in a practical way, their minds are likely to go blank on test day.

I recall helping a student study for her science final in my homeroom. She had a study guide eight pages long and I was asking her the questions. I will give her credit; she could certainly memorize the definitions. However, when I asked Diane to explain them or give me an example, she was unable to do it. She became frustrated and asked me to go on to the next question. When I asked to her to define oxidation, she could tell me it was the combination of a substance with oxygen causing a reaction in which the elements lose electrons, but she could not tell me why the fenders on a car rust. To understand a subject, students need to listen to the teacher every day, ask questions about things they do not understand, do their homework each night, and study week by week. **In short, they must actually work at studying.** Students who choose to merely memorize will often put off studying until the night before the big test and then "cram" for several hours, trying to memorize enough information to get a passing grade. These kids take it easy week after week and then try to achieve a decent grade at the last minute. Ask them throughout the semester if they have any homework and they will probably shake their heads no. Ask them about their grade and they will be evasive and fail to give you a satisfactory answer.

When my daughter was in first grade, her teacher had a test called the mad minute. It covered addition and subtraction facts. Each student was required to write the correct answer to thirty problems in one minute. The tests were organized by numbers: the students could not progress to the fives until they had passed the fours, were not allowed to take the fours until they were perfect on the threes and so on. Before a teacher can introduce math concepts, young students must know their basic facts. One afternoon my first grade daughter and I were having a conversation about how she was doing in school. The subject of math came up and she made a comment that concerned me. She told me she was unable to pass the mad minute. She said she knew the facts but when she sat down to take the test, her mind went blank. I could feel my blood pressure rising. I had heard this excuse from my students many times before and now my own seven-year-old daughter was using it.

We had to put a stop to this immediately. I got out the flash cards and we went up to her room. We took out all the cards with the number she was trying to pass. I repeated her words saying, "You're telling me you know the facts, but when you sit down to take the test your mind goes blank. Is that correct?" She nodded her head. I continued, "Let's see how well you know these facts." I took out the flashcards, mixed up the order, and started to review them with her. I flipped through card after card and she knew only about half of them. It took her two or three seconds to come up with her correct answers. I said, "The reason your mind is going blank is you don't know the answers." When she started in with another excuse, I cut her off. saying, "We are going to sit here and work together on these flashcards until you get them all correct in less than one minute and do it three times in a row. We are not leaving this room until you do it." When the tears started flowing, I told her she might as well dry her eyes because she would not be able to see the cards. It did not take too long before she got them all correct, three times in a row. The next day, when I asked her how she did on the mad minute, she had a smile on her face. She passed with seconds to spare. I do not remember her trying that excuse again. Her little sister happened to be eavesdropping in the next room and figured out she better not try that excuse on Mom or Dad either.

Another potential problem arises when schools put labels on students. I am referring to the different classifications applied to students with learning disabilities. I teach at a high school with over three thousand students. With those numbers, we have our share of kids with learning disabilities. Of course, many of these are legitimate cases who really need the resource teacher's help to succeed in school. However, in recent years, the number of labeled students has been growing at an alarming rate. When coded with a learning disability, some students use it as an excuse for not doing their work. Many of these students could overcome their lack of academic success by developing good study habits.

I had a learning-disabled student in my health class during his sophomore year. He failed the class. George was in my class again in his junior year. He again failed the class. George was enrolled in my class for a third time, but I encouraged him to ask his counselor to put him in another class with a different teacher. I thought someone else might be able to help him. He told me he wanted to stay in my class and was going to do much better this time. When I asked the reason for his attitude adjustment, he said his father was going to buy him a car if he earned an A in the class. This coded student paid attention this time and turned in every homework assignment. He participated in class discussions and stayed awake each day. George asked questions about concepts he did not understand. He did all the extra credit work and even picked up a ten point bonus for perfect attendance. I was not surprised when he got an A on his first test. His effective study habits continued throughout the semester: George earned an A for the class and was given his car. The message to parents who have children with learning disabilities is, "Don't be an enabler. **Don't allow your children to use their coded labels as an excuse to get out of doing their work."** I would also add that a self-motivated student would not need a car as an incentive to make good grades.

The quote from Plato at the beginning of this chapter is worth keeping in mind. When teachers, parents, and students work together, a good education will be the result and it will point the student in the right direction. The advice is as good today as it was long ago. Without the proper support of their parents, many children lose their way on the path to a successful life.

Notes for Chapter Six
How to Raise a Successful Student

Actions speak louder than words.

Chapter Seven
Dependability and Commitment

My older brother owns his own construction company. He has told me that the number of dependable people in his profession is decreasing at a disturbing rate. A growing number of construction professionals agree to undertake work or deliver building materials and then fail to complete the job. The same people lie and miss deadlines on a regular basis. They simply cannot be counted on. From my perspective, this disturbing trend is happening throughout our society. Parents can use this awareness to help their children gain an advantage that will increase their chances of living better lives. When handled properly, this negative trend can be turned into a positive for children. As the number of unreliable people increases, so will the need for individuals who are dependable and follow through on their commitments. People whose word is their bond will be in greater demand than ever before. Value the importance of dependability and commitment and nurture these traits in your children.

In this chapter I will discuss the following points:

- teaching children to be dependable
- determination and trust
- parents who raise reliable kids lay the foundation for learning how to make and keep commitments
- problems created by parents who over-schedule activities
- being a good listener
- supper menu for the week
- advantages to be gained by dependable people who follow through on their commitments, and
- those who talk the talk but do not walk the walk

Two words come to mind when I think of the concept of dependability: determination and trust. The world is full of people who cannot be counted on. **Talk is cheap.** Parents need to teach their kids to do what they say they will do and to finish what they start. Trust is a byproduct of reliability. As other people interact with your kids, they will notice when your children consistently follow through. Trust must be earned. Without trust, any relationship will experience trouble, if it survives at all.

Parents have many opportunities to foster the development of dependability. Recognize and take advantage of these "teachable moments" whenever they occur. When parents do this year after year, slowly but surely reliability is ingrained into their children's moral fiber. Important character traits develop over time; the example set by parents will, once again, be a significant influence.

Let me give you some examples of teachable moments from our family. When our older daughter was in first grade, she decided a dog would be a nice addition to the family. We had planned on getting a dog at some point, and we had a fenced in back yard with plenty of room. Although the timing seemed right, veteran dog owners understand that acquiring a puppy is a significant commitment. The unconditional love between children and their dog is special. My wife and I wanted our girls to experience this unique bond. Further, when kids are expected to care for their dog's daily needs, dependability can be reinforced. When the girls asked us to get a puppy, we sat down and discussed what was involved with dog ownership. The girls agreed to all the conditions without hesitation. My wife and I realized they did not fully understand what they were getting themselves into, but we knew this was all part of the learning process. It was not long before a cute little beagle puppy was welcomed into our family. At first, our girls were ideal dog owners. The novelty began to wear off as the puppy matured into a full-grown dog. Cleaning the water and food bowls along with patrolling the back yard with a "pooper scooper" became never-ending and dreaded chores. We reminded our daughters what they agreed to in our pre-dog discussion and we held them to it. My wife and I emphasized that Boomer depended on them for his daily needs. As time passed, they figured out they would not be able to get out of the work and ended up following through on their commitment to us and our dog. Dog ownership provides several opportunities to learn skills for living. If possible, parents should take advantage of this chance for their kids to learn and grow. If you do make the decision to get a dog, I have one suggestion: do some research to ensure you select a dog whose **size and temperament** match your family's expectations.

At dinner one night, our daughter asked us if she could take piano lessons. Learning to play a musical instrument has many benefits. Our next door neighbor taught music lessons, so, once again, the timing seemed right. We all sat down with the teacher and she patiently explained to our second grade daughter what was involved in learning to play the piano. We would initially purchase an electronic keyboard for practice. We would need to pay for lessons once a week. Sarah would need to practice thirty minutes every day. She would need to commit to two years of this routine before she could expect to make any real progress. We watched Sarah nod her head enthusiastically to each of these conditions. As before, my wife and I knew our daughter did not fully understand what she was taking on. However, if handled properly, we believed this was another experience that would provide us an opportunity to teach commitment. After a month or two, we noticed we were not hearing the keyboard so often. Sarah was beginning to make excuses for not practicing every day. We put a stop to that and reminded her of the promise she had made before we started her lessons.

Quitting was not an option. Just as her teacher had told her, in two years Sarah was making real progress. After that time, she had fulfilled her pledge; then, she could decide what she wanted to do. Sarah voluntarily continued with her piano lessons for three more years. Our younger daughter also took piano lessons. We ended up buying a real piano. Among the many benefits of learning how to play an instrument, making and keeping a commitment may well be the most important of all.

In the summer before sixth grade, our daughter asked me what I thought about her going out for the junior high cross-country team. I have been around sports as an athlete and coach for most of my life, so I explained what she could expect as far as making the team. When I finished, I asked her if she was still interested. She told me she wanted to think it over and would tell me later. I could not help but smile as I remembered how quickly she had agreed to the conditions regarding the commitments of caring for a dog and of taking piano lessons. Once again, I knew she could not fully comprehend what I had told her about cross-country. However, she was beginning to think before she made a decision to say yes or no. She was starting to understand how important her word is to people. A few days later she came to me with her decision. Yes, she wanted to be a part of the junior high cross-country team. We took her to the athletic shoe store to buy some good running shoes. I asked her if she would like to join me when I went jogging three or four times a week. Sarah thought wearing the new shoes and running with Dad sounded like a fun idea. This was all happening in late June when the heat and humidity of summer were becoming uncomfortable. Sarah went jogging with me and we took it slowly and easily. The next time I asked her to join me she came up with an excuse.

These excuses lasted another week and then I stopped asking her to jog with me. The last thought I shared with Sarah on the topic was that she could expect her cross-country practices to be more difficult if she did not do some pre-season conditioning. Life would be wonderful if children always followed their parents' advice. We have a framed saying over our kitchen sink that says, "Dad knows best, but nobody ever listens." I imagine there are many fathers (and mothers) who can relate to that sentiment.

Practice officially started for Sarah in the middle of August. When she came dragging in from her first session, she mumbled something about her sadistic coach trying to torture her. After the second day of running, she did not think she was so interested in being on the cross-country team. By the third day, she was ready to quit. My wife and I then sat her down and informed her that **quitting was not an option.** She would go to every practice and every meet until the season was over. She did not have to run cross-country in seventh grade, but she would be expected to fulfill her commitment to run in sixth grade. August gave way to September and the weather became more comfortable. Sarah's running endurance improved; she found the practices challenging, but no longer torturous. She slept and ate better than she had in a long time. In mid-October, the season ended and we were proud of her. Twenty-four sixth graders showed up for the first day of training. By the end of the season, only four were still on the team. I know this was an important learning experience for our daughter. She never did go out for cross-country again, but she did run on the track team for the next four years. Today, she jogs three or four times a week and I could not begin to keep up with her.

When your children come to you with a serious request or proposal, listen and discuss it before saying yes or no. If there is potential for lessons to be learned that will help them in life, give these requests serious consideration. When you do give your approval, see to it they follow through on their ideas. Whether it is a dog, piano lessons, a sport, or something else, opportunities to teach dependability and commitment will come along and observant parents will take advantage of those occasions. When young children are consistently taught to do what they say they will do, the training carries over until it becomes a way of life. They learn to think before they agree to do something. If they do say yes, they will mean it and follow through.

I overheard a conversation our younger daughter was having with a friend. A classmate of theirs had accepted an invitation to the upcoming dance. When another boy asked her, she cancelled on the first because she liked the second boy more. I heard Betsy say that since this girl had accepted the invitation from the first boy, she should have gone with him to the dance. Breaking that date to go with another boy was just not right. I walked out of eavesdropping range pleased to have learned that our other daughter was also beginning to understand the concept of dependability.

Both of our girls were active in student government at their middle school and high school. Part of their responsibilities involved assisting with orientation programs, school dances, fund-raisers, and convocations. I can remember how frustrated the girls would get when other students who were supposed to be helping out would show up late or not at all. As the months went by, the dependable students stood out from the ones who could not be counted on. The administrators, teachers, and other student leaders quickly figured out which kids were trustworthy. Each time the girls came home complaining, my wife or I would listen as they vented their feelings.

When they finished, we would encourage them to keep working hard. **We told them to live their lives by their own standards and to reject the negative attempts of their peers to drag them down to that level.** We advised them that as long as they could look at themselves in the mirror and feel good about their efforts, they were handling themselves appropriately.

People who keep their word are in greater demand than ever before. In school, these students will receive the best recommendations for jobs and college applications. They will earn the leadership positions. These will be the students who win the honors and awards at the end of the school year. The erratic students will be left empty-handed as they watch the achievers celebrate. Kids who have not learned the importance of reliability and obligations are at the beginning of a long and bumpy road, with failure and disappointment waiting down the line.

Determination is a key component of dependability and commitment. More and more high school students abandon their objectives when they experience adversity. These kids are easily discouraged. They are fine as long as everything is going their way, but as soon as events take a negative turn, so do their attitudes. These students complain, make negative comments to others, put forth half-hearted efforts, and eventually quit. I have seen this happen in the classroom, the weight room, the gym, and on the athletic field. **Kids who become easily discouraged will grow into adults who become easily discouraged.**

Another problem is parents who over-schedule activities which make it difficult if not impossible for their children to demonstrate dependability. Requiring or allowing children to get involved in too many activities outside the school day can be detrimental to the kids as well as to the rest of the family. I agree with psychologist Dr. John Rosemond who wrote in one of his weekly newspaper columns:

> "A family is people growing together, not people running around like chickens with their heads cut off, trying to fulfill arbitrary obligations. Do you want your children to grow up remembering relaxed family evenings, or do you want them remembering that almost every evening was a hurry-up, we gotta go occasion?"

Being over-involved slowly breaks down the closeness of the family. Lines of communication start to deteriorate and family members begin to grow apart from each other. Psychologist Dr. Doris W. Heimering made an excellent point in one of her newspaper columns when she wrote:

> "All of this translates into too much stimulation. Problems then arise, in that a child does not really get to know himself because he has little time to reflect on himself and no time to quietly kick back and dream. And the child also winds up not knowing his parents, grandparents, and siblings. Relationships take a back seat because, for a relationship to develop, people must spend not only activity time but also talk time and quiet time together."

To keep the lines of communication open between the parent and child, a mother and father must develop the important skill of being a good listener. The following example helps make my point and comes from *Creative Brooding* by Robert Raines. It is part of a letter an older teenager wrote to his parents.

> I remember all the nice things you gave me for Christmas and my birthday and I was really happy with the things— about a week, but the rest of the time during the year I really didn't want presents, I just wanted all the time for you to listen to me like I was somebody who felt things too.
>
> Mom, you are a wonderful cook, and you had everything so clean and you were tired so much from doing all those things that made you busy; but, you know something, Mom? I would have liked crackers and peanut butter just as well if you had only sat down with me a while during the day and said to me: "Tell me all about it so I can maybe help you understand."
>
> I think that all the kids who are doing so many things that grown-ups are tearing out their hair worrying about are really looking for somebody that will have time to listen a few minutes and who really and truly will treat them as they would a grown-up who might be useful to them, you know— polite to them."

Being a good listener not only helps your children, but your friends and co-workers as well. **We all need someone we can talk to who will really listen.** If a person cannot express his or her feelings and frustrations to a parent, spouse, friend, co-worker, or relative, it can lead to repression and other potential problems. **Being a good listener takes time** and you cannot rush through it. I am guessing there will be some people who read this and think, what is so hard about listening? Do you not just sit down with the person and listen to what they have to say? In some ways, that is true. However, there is more involved with this ability than just sitting down and listening.

When I was a newlywed, my wife and I were getting ready for another day of teaching, and she started telling me about some problems she was experiencing at her school. She had only made a couple of comments when I interrupted and said, "I'll tell you what you need to do. You should…" Before I could finish telling her what she needed to do, she cut me off with, "Jack, will you just be quiet and listen?" So, I shut up and listened. I learned an important concept about being a good listener. Sometimes people do not want your advice or opinion. Frequently, they just want to express whatever is bothering them because it makes them feel better. Following are a few other ideas I have learned over the years that have been helpful.

One of the toughest obstacles to overcome can be getting the conversation started. You can often sense this initial reluctance to open up from the person's facial expressions and body language. In these situations, I have had success by asking the first question. For instance, "I know you have been going through some tough times. What has been the most difficult part for you?" Another possibility is, "It must be very frustrating for you to be dealing with all these problems." Usually, he or she will start talking and you must then be quiet and pay attention. When questions come up, go ahead and ask them, but make sure you allow the other person ample opportunity to talk. Do not give advice unless asked. Wise people do not need it and fools will not heed it.

We had a saying we used within our family that I saw written on a sign in the Green Bay Packers locker room back in 1969. Vince Lombardi was gone by then, but the sign was left over from his coaching days. The sign said, "What you say here and hear here, let it stay here when you leave here." If you break a person's trust, it is unlikely he or she will confide in you again.

Passing judgment can break down the lines of communication and will cause the child or adult to become angry, or defensive, or shut down. As a parent, I know from experience how easily this can happen. If discussions between parents and kids consistently turn into arguments, children will look elsewhere for people to confide in. When this happens, the alternate confidant may be a negative one.

Credibility is another factor that helps in opening up the lines of communication. To establish credibility, a person must set a good example in his or her own life. Kids can recognize hypocrites quickly and do not respect them. When children do not respect their parents, they will be less likely to confide in them.

Being a good listener is a skill that can have a positive impact on all relationships. Helping others by listening is one of the most satisfying and rewarding acts one person can do for another. However, **it takes time to be a good listener.** When all your time is taken up by over-scheduled activities, communication breaks down and problems can develop.

If children have too many scheduled activities in addition to their school work, they are in danger of "getting too many irons in the fire." For example, soccer practice, Cub Scouts, violin lessons, and baseball practice along with homework will take their toll as the weeks go by. When you factor in additional siblings who are just as busy, the situation can be overwhelming for both the child and the family. Something has to give and the results can be counterproductive. When children are shuttled from one organized activity to another, they miss out on quality developmental experiences of childhood. Playing outside, riding bikes with friends, climbing trees, exploring the creek, lying down in the grass to watch the clouds float by, and playing neighborhood kickball games are sacrificed by over-scheduled children. Creativity and independence are stifled. They simply do not know how to play without adult supervision and direction. Kids with this lifestyle find it difficult to be dependable because they cannot be in two different locations at the same time.

Another potential problem is permitting children to play on two different teams or play more than one sport during the same season. One spring I was coaching baseball and had just completed the selection of our team. With "cuts" over, we began preparing for our opening game. The next day one of the players informed me he could not be at practice because he had a soccer game. I told him that although I liked soccer, he had made a commitment to be a part of our program. As coach, I had cut many other players and selected him for our team, and we were depending on him. I told him he needed to decide if he wanted to play baseball or soccer that spring. I would not allow him to do both because of my belief in the importance of dependability and commitment. He could play organized soccer at any other time of the year, but not during our baseball season. He had a responsibility to his teammates and his coach. Although his parents were upset with me, he decided to play on our baseball team.

When our children chose to play on a sports team, we stressed the importance of attending each practice and game unless there was a good reason not to do so. In other words, unless there was a death in the family or they had a compound fracture, they were expected to be at *all* practices and games. One year our younger daughter was playing on a little league soccer team and two of her teammates upset her and some of the other girls because they rarely, if ever, attended practice, but would show up for the games. They consistently missed practice because they were playing on another soccer team in a different league at the same time. Children who are allowed to participate in such a half-hearted fashion will have more difficulty developing dependability and commitment.

Once activities are limited to manageable levels, parents and children still need organization within the family. Structure contributes toward relaxed evenings at home with quality time together. I would like to share another idea that was helpful to our family when we were going through those times. When our younger child started first grade, my wife went back to work full- time. When she resumed her career as a first grade teacher, I had to take on additional responsibilities around the house. One of those chores was cooking dinner for our family. The head chef also had to expand his role as Dad's Taxi Cab driver. Even when parents limit after school activities to reasonable schedules, they still need to help provide transportation and this can complicate dinner plans. By the time I figured out what I was going to fix for supper, I was usually missing some of the items needed to prepare the meal. So, I had to return to the grocery store or cook something else. Most of us start getting tired at the end of the day and those extra trips back to the grocery store in the late afternoon added to the stress.

There had to be a better way of organizing this situation. So, we came up with what our family called "The Supper Menu for the Week." Breakfast was not much of a problem for us. Juice, cereal, fruit, bagels, toast, and English muffins were the standard choices. Everyone ate lunch at school. Dinner was where the problems developed. I usually did our meal planning on Sunday afternoon. Each family member was allowed to select a dinner for one day. The only requirement was there needed to be a meat, vegetable, and some type of potato, pasta, bread, or rice (complex carbohydrates) included in their choices. After receiving requests from my wife and daughters, I would plan the other two weekday meals myself. Our weekend schedules were too unpredictable to try and set up any definite dinner plans.

Once I had the menu set, I made my grocery list. It did not take long before I figured out how much milk, orange juice, and other basic foods our family would consume in one week. When the menu was organized and the list of necessary supplies complete, I would go to the grocery store. Since I knew ahead of time what was needed for the meals we had planned, I only needed to go to the grocery store once a week. I learned how to group list items together in a time-saving manner. I would start with the produce we needed and then go to the meat counter. Next on the list were the dairy products. After that, I would pick up all the remaining items.

With this system, I never had to worry about what I was cooking for our evening meal. I did not have to make additional trips to the grocery store because I was missing something. I would freeze the meat for the upcoming week. Each morning as I left for work, I would look at our menu posted on the front of the refrigerator and thaw out the meat for dinner that evening. Along with the meal for each day we posted any activity that was scheduled. I would get this information from my wife and kids on Sunday afternoon when we were planning the meals. I would use our family calendar which was also posted on the front of the refrigerator. A typical menu for the week would look like this:

Supper Menu for October 10 to 14

Monday: marinated chicken breast
on Caesar salad
carrot sticks and rolls — Betsy: soccer practice – 4:00

Tuesday: stuffed potatoes
- broccoli, bacon, & cheese — Sarah: piano lesson – 4:30

Wednesday: chef salad - lettuce, tomato,
cucumber, eggs, turkey, ham,
carrots, cheese
French bread — Jack: take out the trash

Thursday:	spaghetti salad – lettuce, tomato, cucumber, carrots	Deb: Betsy:	ADK meeting – 7:00 soccer practice – 4:00
Friday:	pork chops wild rice with mushrooms green beans	Everybody:	football game – 7:30

An added benefit from this system is everyone knew ahead of time what we were having for supper. As a result, the kids did not complain quite so much. The girls always had at least one special meal during the week to look forward to. Since I did the cooking, my wife and daughters cleaned up after dinner, another routine that helped out. This idea was effective in relieving stress and keeping our busy family organized.

Our plan allowed us to sit down and eat dinner together. When activities are limited, families have opportunities to grow together. They will not be trying to fulfill too many obligations. This approach allows children time to focus on schoolwork and their limited activity involvement, which in turn helps foster the development of dependability.

As reliable children grow into adults, the ability to make and keep commitments will be beneficial in many ways. First, consider the impact on their personal lives. Their relationships will improve and remain positive. They will have and be better friends. Quality individuals do not choose as friends or partners those who are unreliable and cannot be trusted. **Surround yourself with good people and good things usually happen.** People who make and keep commitments make better husbands and wives. They will not give up easily and seek a divorce as soon as problems develop. In addition to being better spouses, they will be better parents. When their children are born, they will be committed to providing all the love and support the children need.

Second, consider the positive impact reliability can have on their professional lives. Those who can make and keep commitments will be more respected. They will have more influence on the decision-making process of their jobs. Because they are recognized as dependable, determined, trustworthy, respected, and influential employees, these individuals will enjoy greater success. When promotions are made, they are more likely to be selected and move up to positions of greater responsibility with increased salaries.

Determined people understand the concept of delayed gratification. They have learned to "pay their dues." They set long-term goals and work hard to reach them. They develop a plan for their lives and commit to that plan. Long-term goal-setting also includes the objective of responsible financial management. Such people will live within their means in regards to personal finances.

Being raised by parents who instill dependability and commitment will not guarantee children a charmed life. However, reliable individuals who have the ability to make and deliver on commitments have a much better chance of succeeding than those who do not. In their personal lives, people who are unreliable and cannot be trusted will have more trouble developing lasting friendships. Without good friends, helpful and supportive influences will be missing from their lives.

Those who do not keep commitments make poor marital choices. Once married, their vows mean little if anything. As the inevitable adversity arises in their marriage, they will be more likely to file for divorce. Such people are easily discouraged and quit when the realities of life do not go their way. With their own children, they will be less likely to be supportive and loving parents. The children suffer emotionally and financially because these irresponsible adults refuse to follow through on their obligations to their families.

Think about how the lack of commitment will affect people's professional lives. Such people are simply not in demand: few if any employers want them. As a result, they never seem to get ahead. Some become bitter people who consistently rationalize their shortcomings and fail to improve. **When their professional disappointments are combined with their personal problems the result is lives of frustration and unhappiness.**

Kids are not born with the innate ability to keep their word. Parents who fail to teach this skill for living set them up for failure and disappointment. When young children are taught to be dependable, they are more likely to grow into trustworthy teenagers and determined adults capable of making and keeping commitments. These qualities will help them become successful both personally and professionally.

Notes for Chapter Seven
Dependability and Commitment

Notes for Chapter Seven
Dependability and Commitment

Students should get involved with extra-curricular activities for the reward, not the award.

~ Eric Clark

Chapter Eight
Extra-Curricular Activities

Getting involved in extra-curricular activities should be encouraged as parents guide their children through the teenage years. I have been a teacher, coach, and club sponsor for over thirty years. In that time I have observed many students who genuinely enjoyed school. Unfortunately, I have seen too many who disliked school and could not wait to leave. These are the students who watch the clock on the classroom wall and anxiously await the bell that signals the end of another period. They ignore the sign I have next to my clock that reads, "Don't count the minutes— make the minutes count." For these unhappy students, time moves agonizingly slow. For these students school is boring. They tell you their teachers are boring, their families are boring, and even their city is boring. I tell them **boring people get bored.** They labor through each school day giving the impression they are in a prison. At three o'clock they finally get their wish and the school day ends. At this point these kids will either go to work at part-time jobs (usually to enable them to pay for their cars), sleep, talk on the telephone, watch television, play video games, listen to music or go to the mall and "chill with their friends." Why do some kids enjoy school and others dread it? One reason involves extra-curricular activities.

In this chapter I will discuss the following points:

- benefits to be gained by children participating in extra-curricular activities
- understanding the degree of commitment required to participate: substantial to limited
- ways parents can enhance the activity for their child, and

- actions by parents which detract from their child's experience.

Some parents may wonder if participating in extra-curricular activities can really make much of a difference to their child's development. Can such activity be a determining factor in whether or not students have a positive or negative school experience? My answer is an unequivocal YES. Let me give an example which helps make my point. A young man in one of my elective weight-training classes during the first semester of his junior year had a bad attitude and did not like school. Mike did not appear to have any friends. He complained, made derogatory comments to classmates, put forth a half-hearted effort and would occasionally be disrespectful to me. Mike was demonstrating the same behavior in his other classes. When the first semester ended I felt sorry for him, but I was glad to see him go. When we received our student rosters for second semester I was surprised to see Mike had signed up to take my course again. Before the bell rang one day, he asked me what I thought about his going out for the rugby team. I was pleasantly surprised and told him I thought it was a great idea. Mike confided he had never played rugby. I informed him his lack of experience would not prevent him from making the team. There were no "cuts" in rugby and there was a reserve team in addition to the varsity squad. I assured him that if he maintained a good attitude, he would be fine.

Mike joined the rugby team. As we progressed through the second semester I noticed several interesting changes in this young man. He would talk with a couple of other boys in weight-training and also on the rugby team about practices and games. Girls like to watch the games and as the season came to an end I noticed Mike now had a girlfriend.

Paralleling these developments in rugby were positive changes in Mike's attitude toward school. He had made new friends from the team. Mike looked forward to school and seeing his girlfriend. He had fun playing rugby and he felt part of something special that was connected to our school. These newfound interests carried over into his schoolwork. Mike stopped complaining and started making a sincere effort. His second semester grades improved in all of his classes. In short, his whole attitude towards school changed because of his participation in an extra-curricular activity. Mike's academic and athletic improvement continued and he genuinely enjoyed his senior year.

All students need to find at least one extra-curricular activity in which they can develop an interest. This is especially true at a large school. Kids need to find their niche so that a big school seems smaller. As parents see their children showing an interest they need to be supportive and offer encouragement. When kids get involved for the **reward,** their motivation and expectations are soundly based. When they participate for the **award,** the students are participating for selfish reasons. As students consider which activities they might participate in they also need to understand the level of commitment involved.

What will be expected is based in part on the activity itself. Another significant factor is the leadership style of the coach, director or sponsor. Extra-curricular activities requiring a substantial commitment offer the most potential benefits. Competitive programs such as the school's top show choir, orchestra, marching band and varsity athletic teams are all extra-curricular activities in which the students are being motivated by coaches and directors to levels of achievement they probably would not reach on their own. The kids learn an effective approach to preparation for competition. They will carry the same methods over into their adult lives. The traits that allow students to develop into successful musicians, actors, singers and athletes will be the same as those to be found in successful health professionals, business men and women, teachers and lawyers. These are qualities such as sportsmanship, strong work ethic, teamwork, understanding your role, responsibility, goal-setting, dealing with adversity, satisfying a need to belong by being a part of something special, paying your dues, mental toughness, selflessness, loyalty, priority setting, and time management.

The lessons learned from highly competitive activities where a substantial commitment of time and effort is expected are immeasurable. Many years ago I heard this view expressed by a player on one of Vince Lombardi's Green Bay Packers championship teams of the 1960s. The athlete believed that through such learning experiences people move inside a circle of winners. Once individuals have been inside that circle they are never content to be outside it. I believe he was saying that the circle of winners symbolizes the success which comes from making a commitment to excellence. Children should do the best they can at whatever they decide to do. They need to find an extra-curricular activity that matches their interests and strengths and then put their hearts into it. Success is then just a matter of time. When repeated over and over this becomes a way of life.

All students in these competitive programs will experience some type of failure and, without doubt, make mistakes. This is all part of the learning process. Miscues will usually be followed by constructive criticism from the coach or director. Occasionally, the leader's voice may reach a decibel level where some of the students perceive they are being yelled at. Some kids may react inappropriately to constructive criticism. They feel they are being singled out and picked on. They make excuses. Their facial expressions clearly convey what they are feeling inside: how dare you raise your voice to me! Some even go so far as to make disrespectful verbal replies. Hopefully, the students eventually figure out that the leader is trying to help them improve. If they persist long enough these thin-skinned students may progress to a point where they can listen to the critique, improve, and become part of the program. Failure to do so results in loss of playing time or a diminished role. For some young people this is a valuable lesson.

Many students do not take advantage of the variety of programs and activities offered by their schools. They consequently fail to learn and grow through the life lessons associated with these opportunities. These students have not developed the self-confidence necessary for the occasions when their shortcomings are objectively evaluated by the adults in their lives. What will happen to these same students when they become adults and their boss at work expresses his or her expectations for improvement? These people could be married and have families depending on them to bring home their paychecks. If they lose their tempers, quit their jobs or get fired, then their families suffer. If they become defensive or withdrawn, they will be unlikely to improve professionally.

David Brooks wrote an article that appeared in *Men's Health* magazine which he titled, "Where Pride Still Matters." I thought he did a great job of sharing the benefits to be gained by playing on athletic teams. One of his points is appropriate for the topic of dealing with mistakes and failures. He wrote:

> "Sports involve suffering. Grade inflation being what it is, and the self-esteem ethic being what it is, lots of kids can go through school and other parts of their lives without ever having to deal with humiliating failure. Everybody is above average. But in sports there is no escaping failure.

> In baseball you strike out, you walk in a run, you drop a ball. And you don't confront failure in the privacy of a small conference room or on a confidential report card. It happens to you on the field, in front of everybody."

Learning to deal with failure and constructive criticism makes students emotionally stronger and helps prepare them for dealing with future bosses.

Our daughter had a part-time job working for a company that catered for weddings, parties and business programs. On one occasion she was assisting with one of the biggest events of the year, a party on the night before the Indianapolis 500 Race at the home of one of the wealthiest men in our city. Several hundred people were to attend the party, including many celebrities in town for the big race. Sarah's boss was under a great deal of stress and, when things did not go according to plan, he took his group aside and into one of the nearby tents. He issued some strong demands of the workers. When he left the tent a number of the helpers were visibly shaken. Several of the girls were actually crying. From the caterer's perspective everything from that point went well and the party was a success. As the group began cleaning up the boss began to feel a little guilty about his comments in the tent before the party. He went around to each worker and apologized for losing his temper. When he spoke with our daughter she said, "That's nothing. You should see my dad when he gets mad." I am not advocating a leader yelling at his team or group whenever complications arise, but children need to be prepared so that when the inevitable criticism happens they have learned to listen and make the necessary adjustments. If they do not have this mental toughness then kids may start crying, quit, mouth off, or shut down because they are unable to handle the personal appraisal.

Participating in activities where a limited commitment is expected also offers opportunities that students should explore. Some students are not willing to attend structured practices every day after school, do what is expected during the off-season to remain on the team, or give up weekends and vacations for competition and more practices. There are still plenty of suitable activities from which to choose. Depending on the leadership, sponsors might have the students meet once a month, bi-monthly, once a week or several times a week for a limited time. Students need to seek out this information and decide whether they are willing to conform to the leader's expectations. Examples of less-demanding activities include French Club, intramural and club sports, Academic Decathlon, Key Club, African-American Scholars, Diner's Club, and the Speech Team. All of these offer chances to make new friends, develop a feeling of connection with the school, as well as learn skills for living. One of the many advantages of a big school is the wide variety of organized activities to choose from.

Student government offers yet another option for interested students. Varying levels of commitment will be required depending on the amount of responsibility students are willing to accept. Some positions are elected but others are filled by appointment. President, vice-president, secretary, treasurer, committee chairperson or committee member of a school government body are all important positions available to anyone interested. Student government offers these leaders the chance to help organize convocations, fund raisers, dances and other activities that form an integral part of the school year.

Friendships are vital for a positive school experience. Students need to have friends they look forward to seeing when they arrive at school. Kids need to share movies, games, dances, plays, concerts, and daily activities with friends. Quality friendships are much more likely to develop during after-school activities than they are in the classroom. Involvement allows kids an opportunity to meet new people and add to their circle of neighborhood, grade school and middle school contacts.

Students create many of their most valued memories while participating in extra-curricular activities. At my own class reunions, as well as those of former students, most of the memories shared and stories told are associated with some type of extra-curricular activity.

A long-term benefit of participation in extra-curricular activities is the boost they provide when it comes to college and job applications. University admission officers and potential employers are looking for involved students. These people know about the benefits derived from participation in these programs. References are also an important component of this process. Students are usually required to include with their applications at least three credible references. Letters of recommendation from coaches, directors and sponsors can be valuable supplements to those from teachers and counselors.

At the beginning of each semester I spend time getting to know my students. I write the following points on the board for them to share with our class: name, grade school, middle school, hobbies, extra-curricular activities, favorite movie / book / television show / singer or group / subject; if I could relive one moment of my life it would be...; and repeat their name. As the years have gone by I have seen a sad and disturbing trend in an increasing number of my students. Some of them have moved so many times that by their teenage years they cannot even remember all their schools' names. I can still recall the names of all my elementary teachers and I am guessing many adults reading this can do the same. A growing number of students list the following as their only hobbies: sleeping, talking on the telephone, watching television, and hanging out with their friends. I have heard as much as half the class admit they do not participate in any extra-curricular activities. They say they need to work after school or just want to hurry home at three o'clock and take a break. As they continue down the list many of these same students do not have a favorite book because they do not like to read. They do not have a favorite subject in school or a moment from their past which they would relive if given the chance. These are the uninvolved and bored students who do not enjoy school. I am not suggesting extra-curricular activities would magically reverse these apathetic attitudes but **I have witnessed some amazing transformations in the outlook of students who made the decision to get involved.**

College applications are another problem uninvolved kids will have to face during their senior year. Who will be their references? Who will write their letters of recommendation? Will there be a university eager to welcome them as incoming freshmen? These students are probably in for a rude awakening.

Kids have many of the same doubts and insecurities their parents had as students. Use this insight as a guide when relating to your children. Think back and try to put yourself in their shoes. Be supportive and encourage your kids to get involved at their school. Teenagers can have vulnerable egos and their fear of failure is real. In their minds the safest place to be is on the sidelines. Low self-esteem can intensify their reluctance to voluntarily expose themselves to the possibility of failure. One mistake a person can make is to be afraid of making mistakes. Participation in some activities will put children's egos to the test because obstacles, failures and disappointments go along with the good times. Expect and challenge your children to do their best and then let the chips fall where they may. Remember to reinforce the three-step process for turning mistakes into positive learning experiences: admit the mistake, learn from it, and do not repeat it. Accept that your kids may not become the stars, earn the big scholarships or get their names and pictures in the paper. The parents of the team manager for the basketball team can be just as proud of their child as the parents of the star point guard. Not everyone can be the hero. Someone has to be there on the sidewalk and wave as the heroes pass by. If your child excels, that is great. If not, by participating they still learn valuable skills for living. **Involvement for the right reasons takes much of the pressure off students and allows them to reap the benefits of participating in the activity— and have fun in the process.** It is important for parents to understand this concept; otherwise their influence may have a detrimental effect on their children's experience.

I used to tell my players that one can learn as much about people by observing how they deal with adversity as how they handle success. When you are successful and everything is going your way, life is sweet. What happens when problems arise? As Rev. Robert Schuller said, "Tough times never last, but tough people do." Teaching their children how to deal with adversity in a productive way is one of the most important lessons parents can impart. Once this foundation is in place the schools can build upon it.

Most athletes feel they should be in the starting line-up. Most singers, dancers, musicians, actors and actresses believe they should get the best roles. Some will complain to anyone who will listen. Parents need to understand that coaches want to win. Directors want to put on the best quality performance possible. Coaches see their athletes in practice every day. Directors evaluate their performers daily and match abilities to roles. Listen as your children vent their frustrations. After the kids have had their say, tell them you understand how they feel. We have all been in similar situations. We do know how they feel. **What parents should say next is crucial.** Tell them to hang in there and that quitting is not an option. Make it clear that they do not have to participate in the activity next year, but this year they must finish what they started. Tell them to pay attention so that if an opportunity arises they will be ready to take advantage of it, to keep their mouths shut and their eyes and ears open, and work hard. Tell them to do the best they can at whatever role they are given, stay positive and be a team player. Tell them that when they continue to do these things, if they have the ability, sooner or later the coach or director will notice and they will get their chance. When their chance comes they should give it their best shot. Then they can live with the outcomes and have few regrets.

Getting "cut" from a team or group is tough. Losing a big game after expending maximum effort is tough. Striking out, fumbling the ball or missing the free throw that would have won the game is tough. Suffering these indignities in front of a crowd is tougher still. **Sometimes life is tough and kids had better learn to deal with it.** Of course kids are going to hurt in those situations. As parents, we suffer when our kids suffer. However, as long as parents do not overreact kids will bounce back and get over the emotional pain. I think most of us know all too well how much it hurts to fall short of a goal that you put your heart and soul into achieving. These difficult times may not be life or death but they are significant when they happen to you. Tell your kids you are still proud of them, that you love them, and you know how they feel. Share a candid example of when you went through a similar tough time so they know you really do relate. Tell them time has a way of taking away much of the hurt, life goes on and we still have to get up the next day and go back to work. Going through the bad times allows us to have a greater appreciation of the good times.

Even after you have told your kids all the right things they might still need something extra. Try sharing this quote from Teddy Roosevelt.

Theodore Roosevelt / Twenty-Sixth President

> It is not the critic who counts, not the man who points out how the strong man stumbles or where the doer of deeds could have done them better. The credit belongs to the man who is actually in the arena, whose face is marred by dust and sweat and blood, who strives valiantly, who errs and comes short again and again because there is no effort without error and shortcomings, who knows the great devotion, who spends himself in a worthy cause, who at best knows in the end the high achievement of triumph and who at worst, if he fails while daring greatly, knows his place shall never be with those timid and cold souls who know neither victory nor defeat.

These can be uplifting words for people who are hurting. My grandma used to say, "You can't keep a good man down. You can't keep a good woman down. Good people will bounce back up." We want our kids to learn from their experiences of failure or falling short, become a little stronger with each "scar," and move on to bigger and better things.

A choir director at my school suggests that parents **be supportive from a distance.** During the teenage years kids are starting to break away from their parents. This developing independence is a normal part of growing up. However, at the same time teenagers are beginning to strike out on their own they still want and need the love and approval of their parents. Unless parents have a legitimate excuse they need to be there to support their kids whenever they are involved in a game or performance. Attendance will also help keep the lines of communication open because, by being there, parents will have more to discuss with their children.

The success that follows hard work is satisfying, fun, stimulating, and admirable. Kids and parents should be proud. Many students have learned what it takes to succeed but some of those same students have not learned how to handle success with class. They need to be taught the meaning of humility. Impress upon your kids that when they are truly good at something they do not need to tell people. The grapevine is very efficient. As our daughters went through school and started to succeed we told them that it is nice to be important but it is more important to be nice; always remember the Golden Rule and never look down on anybody unless you are helping them up.

No one likes arrogance. People resent being looked down upon and they do not respect those who believe they are better than everyone else. As time passes the only people who choose to associate with such snobs will probably be the groupies who have their own selfish reasons. As soon as the prima donnas stop succeeding these so-called friends will disappear and, like parasites, go looking for another rising star to latch onto. So, when parents start to sense their children may be getting a little too full of themselves, it is important that they help their kids keep their success in proper perspective.

Guide your children so they grow into quietly confident people who conduct themselves with class wherever they go and in whatever they do. In a poem titled *What Is Class?*, a poet wrote that people with class are confident, do not make excuses, are considerate of others, have good manners, never try to build themselves up by tearing others down, and are comfortable with themselves. The poet went on to write that if you have class, you do not need much of anything else. If you do not have it, no matter what else you have—it does not make much difference.

A few years ago I was talking to a high school swimming coach about how parents can be a detriment to their children's experience in extra-curricular activities. This veteran coach agreed with me and shared a comment made to him by the legendary swim coach from Indiana University – James ("Doc") Councilman. Doc told him his ideal job would be the swimming coach at an orphanage. Parents should take note of this statement from a former Big Ten and Olympic coach. I can tell you from experience that there are times when parents can make teaching and coaching very unpleasant. Most people would not think of walking in and telling a doctor or businessperson how to do his or her job. Yet, some parents do not hesitate to tell a coach or teacher what they should be doing. The same parents can be openly critical whenever they disagree with decisions being made. Their consistent stream of negative comments can have an effect on their children's attitudes. I have come to the conclusion that, deep down, many over-aggressive parents believe they could do a better job teaching or coaching than the people actually in these roles. In a few cases, that may be true. However, we all had a choice as to what career each of us would pursue. I have concluded that many men wish they could have been a coach. They chose a different profession but never got over this unfulfilled desire. Some have coached in Little League sports. However, in their minds, that is not the same thing as middle school or coaching at the high school varsity level. This frustration can lead them to say and do things that are counterproductive.

When children come home complaining about the coach or director, parents should listen but try to remain as neutral as possible. They are only getting one side of the story. I can assure parents the coach's or director's version of events is frequently very different from the student's version. Directors and coaches cannot always be available to sit down with parents each time their kids have a problem. Parents should pick their battles carefully and only intervene when absolutely necessary.

Let me give some examples of over-involved parents. I had a player whose father was always hanging around practice. This man was friendly at first but as the season progressed he became more aggressive. After practices and games the father started coming into our locker room. He continually wanted to know why his son was not getting more playing time. I had already patiently explained my reasoning several times. When he once more came up to me, I decided to get this obnoxious man's attention with some stronger words. He never bothered me again.

At the conclusion of the football season this boy became a member of the basketball team. His father started making the same mistakes with the basketball coaches as he had with me during the football season. During a game-film session, while one of the coaches was telling the man's son what he was doing wrong, the boy stated that he was going to do it his way and the coach was wrong. This player had great potential. Unfortunately, the father's influence was affecting his son's attitude. The coaches kicked this boy off the basketball team. He transferred to another school and the last I heard the father was interfering with the coaches at the new school. If this father had been supportive from a distance his son would have eventually become a starting forward on the varsity basketball team.

Many opportunities to help support extra-curricular activities are available for interested parents. Booster clubs, fundraisers, mothers' clubs, banquet set-up and concession stand workers are ways parents can help. Coaches and directors appreciate such assistance as long as the volunteers are helping for the right reasons. Some parents get involved for the primary purpose of promoting their own children. Some even start telling the coaches and directors what they should and should not do and play Monday Morning Quarterback by second-guessing the leader to anyone who will listen. A choir director at our school told me about a parent volunteer who offered to pay for her and her family to fly to Hawaii if the director would select her daughter for the top group. When the director rejected the offer and "cut" the girl from the group, the parents were upset and criticized the director throughout the community. They could not accept the fact that their daughter was not selected that year because she was not good enough.

Veteran coaches and directors hope to have parent volunteers they can trust. They know that serious problems can occur when selfish parents get involved. One instance of such problems occurred at a high school in central Indiana. The parents shared the job of president for a performing arts booster club. Their son was a senior and had been elected president of the top show choir. Preparations were under way for an upcoming competition. The director was making her evaluations prior to choosing the soloists. She received a lengthy e-mail from the senior boy's parents describing in detail why she should select their son for the coveted solo. As practice continued she decided a sophomore boy would get the part. When the night of the performance arrived everything seemed fine, but unknown to the director, the senior boy had a private conversation with the sophomore soloist. He took him to the corner of the dressing room and informed the underclassman that he was not going to sing the solo. When the time came for him to walk up to the microphone he was to stay in line. The performance was progressing nicely until the senior calmly walked up to the front of the group and sang the solo.

The angry director had her back to a large crowd and decided to deal with this problem when the competition was over. When she found out what had happened she kicked her senior president out of the choir for insubordination. On the following Monday morning she was called to the principal's office where the boy, his parents, and the principal were waiting to discuss the situation. The boy would not apologize because he did not feel he had done anything wrong. His parents agreed with him and demanded the principal reinstate their son immediately. The principal backed up the choir director. As the parents angrily stormed out of the office with their son, they threatened a lawsuit.

Teenage students strive to develop independence, but some parents have trouble relinquishing control. A teacher at our school who gives private voice lessons told me about a mother who sat in on lessons with her teenage daughter. Each time he tried to instruct the girl she looked over to her mother for assurance that it was okay to follow the teacher's directions. The mother was trying to control her daughter and it was working. The teacher told me the girl failed to improve because she listened to her mother instead of to him. He stopped giving her lessons because the mother refused to allow him to work with the girl without interference.

Getting involved for the wrong reasons will usually result in frustration and disappointment. Here is an example of what I mean. A young boy demonstrated that he was a good baseball player. He loved the game and his parents were proud of him. As he went through the Little League years everything went well. During the boy's middle school years his parents' outlook on baseball changed as they started thinking about a college scholarship. The parents pushed the boy to play in leagues and travel teams during the spring and summer. When he was thirteen and fourteen years old he was playing in 50 to

60 games a season. The coaches of these teams welcomed him because of his ability. The parents traveled to see him play. They spent large sums of money staying in hotels, eating at restaurants and driving their car all over the Midwest. During the winter they paid a personal trainer to increase the boy's strength, speed, and flexibility. They hired a personal coach to work with him on his hitting, fielding, and throwing fundamentals. The parents were not wealthy, but in their minds this was an investment. They believed their son's baseball ability would pay for his college education. Each season the boy's enthusiasm for baseball diminished.

He had matured early and during the Little League years he was bigger, stronger, and faster than the other kids. When he reached his freshman and sophomore years of high school many of the other boys were catching up or passing him in physical development. As his interest in baseball started to decline his parents' interest intensified. These people had spent a great deal of time and money; they expected that venture to pay dividends in the form of a "free" college education. The boy had an unimpressive junior season. He made the varsity team, but his playing time was limited. In his senior year he did not make the team and his parents were very upset. They complained about all the money they had wasted on hotels and other traveling expenses. They complained about the time they had spent driving throughout the Midwest to sit there weekend after weekend and tournament after tournament watching baseball games. They complained about how expensive college was going to be for their son without a scholarship. They ended up ruining the baseball experience. Remember the advice at the beginning of this chapter: **students should participate in extra-curricular activities for the reward, not the award.**

Our daughters were fortunate to have the opportunity to attend an excellent high school. Dr. Bill Duke was the principal at the time Sarah and Betsy were students. Bill was a strong supporter of extra-curricular activities. In his view:

> "One of the toughest things for a young person to do is to develop a real sense of accountability and a realistic perspective of the future. Students who are involved in extra-curricular programs understand accountability very quickly because it is immediate in those activities. This is just one of the reasons I believe so strongly in athletic and other extra-curricular programs. They are fundamental in helping students develop the self-discipline necessary to be successful in academics and in later life."

Notes for Chapter Eight
Extra-curricular Activities

Notes for Chapter Eight
Extra-curricular Activities

Your children will be exposed to drugs and you will not be there when it happens.

~ Connie Hines

Chapter Nine
Drugs

I introduce the drug unit of my high school Wellness class by sharing the following fable. A young man enjoyed backpacking and decided he would hike to the top of the mountain close to his home. He parked his car in the valley and started out at sunrise. By noon the hiker had reached the top of the mountain. He sat down to rest, eat lunch and take in the beautiful view. As the afternoon wore on he packed up and headed down the trail, intending to return to his car by sunset. During his descent the young man was surprised by a poisonous snake coiled up alongside the path. The snake looked up at the hiker and said, "Please take me with you to the warm valley below. I'm cold-blooded and will freeze to death if I stay up here."

The backpacker was not sure what to do. He knew this was a dangerous snake but he did not want the snake to die. After thinking the situation over he decided to save the reptile. The young man picked up the snake, put it in his backpack and continued down the mountain. At dusk, as he approached his car, the tired hiker remembered the poisonous snake still in his backpack. He was releasing the reptile when, without warning, the snake sank its fangs deep into his arm with a fatal bite. The shocked backpacker fell to the ground in disbelief. As the young man lay there trying to maintain consciousness he looked at the snake and said, "I saved your life. Why would you do this to me?" The snake looked back and answered, "You knew what I was when you picked me up." The snake slithered away into the warm grass of the valley and the hiker died.

When I ask my students about the moral of the story we have an interesting discussion. I follow up by saying, "After we complete this unit of study, the potential danger of drug abuse should be clear to you. In spite of that knowledge, if any of you still choose to abuse drugs, it will be like picking up a poisonous snake. Sooner or later, that snake is going to bite you."

Involvement with drugs can mean involvement with people who are like that poisonous snake. Positive values do not guide the decision-making process of drug dealers. These people look at life differently from people trying to make an honest living. **It is no coincidence that when drugs are involved there can be violence as well.** Drug dealers do not care about the people who are robbed, injured, and killed. They do not care about overdoses or the fact that the drugs they sell sometimes have chemicals added to the original drugs making them even more dangerous. I remind my students that illegal drugs are not processed under the supervision of a qualified pharmacist. With all of the designer drugs being produced in home laboratories today kids have no way of knowing what they are purchasing. Dealers are not concerned that much of today's crime is directly or indirectly related to drugs. They care about money, which they frequently require to feed their own habits. Of course, dealers would be out of business if nobody purchased their drugs. Unfortunately, business in the illegal drug trade is thriving, with no signs of letting up.

Students have several different reactions to my comments. Some are receptive. Others are not certain what to think, are apathetic, or become defensive. Those kids who are receptive are the ones who have chosen to be drug free. The kids who seem unsure are probably experimenting with occasional drug use but have not progressed to the next level yet. The apathetic kids are seriously into drugs. The kids who become defensive may be seriously into drugs or, possibly, they have people in their lives who deal drugs for the easy money. In recent years some of these students have become very open and will tell our class about cousins, uncles, aunts, and siblings who deal drugs. I would wager a few could add their parents to the list, as well. These students rationalize their relatives' activities because they say they need the money. The end justifies the means and they see nothing wrong with that lifestyle.

Of all the topics I cover in the Wellness course the drug unit is the most frustrating and depressing. How can a teacher talk kids out of using drugs when the adults in their lives are abusing or dealing drugs? I hear about parents who smoke marijuana with their own children. This class helps convince a few kids who are abusing drugs to stop. I know this because they tell me. Unfortunately, most high school students who are abusing drugs are in denial or could care less what a teacher says. A health class will effect little, if any, significant change in their lifestyles. At the high school level our biggest influence is on the kids who are drug free. We reassure them that they are on the right path and reinforce what their parents and teachers have been telling them all along. These classes can also impact the kids at the experimental stage who are still open-minded about the risks. However, adults cannot wait until the high school years to begin educating kids about the dangers of drug abuse. **Parents must begin this process during the early years of elementary school, if not sooner.**

This chapter will be organized into three parts. I will describe for parents what is at risk, explain why kids choose to abuse drugs, and explore a proactive approach that offers advice on how to prevent this from happening in their families.

What is at risk?

Most of today's parents have witnessed young people develop problems as a result of drug abuse. Nevertheless, they may not be fully aware of how serious these problems can be from a practical perspective. I will share some examples of what can happen when parents fail to do what is within their power to raise drug-free children. As a high school teacher I interact with parents and students every day. I have interviewed some of these people to enable me to offer a realistic picture of what can happen. I must say, it is a sobering picture.

Home should be a place to which both children and parents are able to return at the end of the day for rest, relaxation and simply getting away from the stress of everyday life. Students have talked openly to me about the devastating effects of drug abuse on their families and homes. One student, whose sibling was an abuser, said his parents dreaded coming home each night after a tough day at work. They knew there would be yelling and fighting. As the parents continually disagreed about what to do with their child who was abusing drugs, the marriage began to unravel. For younger children, witnessing their mother and father fighting can be a frightening experience. One sibling of an abuser told me, "My brother knew exactly what buttons to push to get my father to lose his temper." This teenage abuser had an underlying anger and resentment toward his parents and took satisfaction from upsetting and hurting them.

The closeness of the family is disrupted as the users isolate themselves from everyone they cared about. In the words of one teenager, "This snowballed until there was a complete breakdown within my family." Parents who must endure this suffer both mentally and physically. When parents do not get a good night's sleep night after night, they never feel right. Their physical condition carries over into their work performance. They lack energy and enthusiasm. They become negative in their outlook toward life in general. One tired parent told me, "I started to doubt myself. I began to second-guess my decisions. My self-confidence was very low and I was totally exhausted."

Some parents cannot sleep because they worry about strangers, users and dealers or police calling or coming to their homes at all hours of the night. Others are justifiably concerned about their teenage abuser stealing from family members. Parents can feel threatened and worry that their own child may physically harm them if they let their guard down and go to sleep. One parent made the following comment after her teenage son was locked-up in jail for a drug offense: "I could finally get a good night's sleep because I knew where he was and knew he could not hurt me or the rest of our family."

Any time someone has a drug problem the whole family is affected. None of us would choose to have our "dirty laundry" displayed for all the neighbors to see. As families do their best to deal with drug-related problems, word gets out and neighborhood grapevines spread local gossip. One student explained how much it hurt her feelings to see her family's reputation tarnished as a result of the trouble they were going through. She confided that the situation degenerated to the point where other neighbors would not allow their children to come over to her house or even associate with her.

Children need their share of privacy just as we all need a space to call our own. For most kids this personal area is their bedroom. One boy I spoke with shared a bedroom with his older brother who abused drugs, including alcohol. When the older brother had too much to drink he would vomit in their bedroom. As time passed the younger brother could not stand to go into his own bedroom. He became very angry as he described the repulsive conditions. In a related story a parent noticed an unpleasant odor coming from his basement. His son was an abuser and would hang out in their basement with his friends. That area of their home did not have a bathroom. The kids were getting high and urinating in the dehumidifier's holding tank. They could have cared less about the odor; some of them even thought it was funny.

At some point things become so bad that parents finally realize they must intervene. A mother told me that putting her son in a treatment program was the most difficult step she ever had to take in her entire life. It hurt one parent to be second-guessed and even judged negatively by so-called friends about the way he had raised his son. In his words, "You are already feeling bad enough and then negative comments from people you thought cared about you make it even worse." For another parent, calling the police to arrest her own child followed by the police car pulling into their driveway was heartbreaking.

In addition to dealing with the emotional aspect of this problem parents must also face the reality of the financial burdens. As one father expressed it to me, "Parents in this situation had better be ready to pay big bucks and prepare for a serious financial drain." A drug counselor informed me that she has seen families forced to re-mortgage their houses to pay the bills for their children's drug treatment programs.

When the family is forced to make financial sacrifices, resentments can build and add more stress to an already difficult situation. A father confided how angry his kids became when their requests had to be turned down because the parents spent all their extra money on treatment for the sibling in trouble with drugs. Children can find it difficult to accept that even though they are "being good," they are penalized in favor of the sibling in trouble. This is a tough way for kids to learn that life is not always fair.

As drug abuse progresses from experimental to social to regular use and possible addiction, so too does the cost of buying drugs. Part-time jobs do not pay enough to keep up with the increasing demand. Teenagers often make more bad decisions as they try to finance their new user lifestyles. Students use words like "snowballed" and "downward spiral" as they describe those who cross over the line from occasional use to abuse. **Stealing and dealing** can become part of the drug abuser's life. These teenagers will steal from stores, neighbors, and even their own families to buy more drugs.

Additional ways kids get their drugs include bartering. Parents need to be aware of this trading network. Students taking prescription Ritalin (or who have access to Ritalin through a sibling) will trade with other abusers for a drug they wish to acquire. Some steal a test from a teacher and trade the test to a student in that class for drugs. Others shoplift items such as CDs to exchange for drugs. Teenage girls prostitute themselves to make money for drugs. Some of these teenagers get caught by the police and add yet another issue for their families to deal with. The cost of hiring a defense lawyer is then added to drug treatment costs; the snowball just gets larger and larger.

Students and parents give additional examples of the liabilities of drug abuse, including:

- car accidents and DUI arrests, increasing car insurance costs
- fights and beatings because the kids were in the wrong place at the wrong time (injuries)
- when drunk or high, kids vandalize property
- lost eligibility for extracurricular activities
- trips to the ER from overdoses and drugs with other chemicals added (marijuana laced with speed, cocaine cut with PCP)
- lower grades in school
- expulsion from school
- rape

- unplanned pregnancy, and
- missing out on the joys of growing up – for example: school dances, clubs, intramural sports, varsity athletic teams, performing arts groups, and development of true friendships that can last a lifetime.

A high school student told me about his childhood, when his big brother was his hero. He looked up to his role model and wanted to be just like him. His brother became a drug abuser and as he sank deeper and deeper into abuse their close relationship spiraled downward. He spoke to me about his disappointment, disillusionment, anger, and feelings of abandonment. The relationship finally tore apart when the younger brother found out his hero was stealing from him in order to buy more drugs. I could see the sadness in his eyes as he said, "At that point, in my mind I lost my brother."

Parents must do everything within their power to guide their children away from drug use. A teenager who makes the decision to experiment with drugs has picked up a poisonous snake that will eventually bite. This mistake will adversely affect all the members of his or her family— physically, emotionally, and financially.

Why do kids abuse drugs?

I have asked kids why they chose to get involved with drugs and found teenagers are very willing to discuss this topic. One student said, "Kids really do want to talk but parents don't really want to listen. They just want to give advice." Teenagers figure if parents will not listen to them why should they listen to their parents? We all need someone to listen to us as we vent our frustrations about things in our lives that worry, bother, and concern us. **Parents who do not sit down and listen to their children on a regular basis may be in for**

serious trouble later. When all is said and done, it is not a great deal for a teenager to ask of his or her parents.

Kids also told me they want to fit in and be a part of a group. One student explained, "Drugs make it easy to fit in because drugs level out the playing field." Cliques are common among middle school and high school students. Drug abuse becomes the **common denominator** that makes acceptance to the same groups almost a certainty. Students with low self-esteem can in this way temporarily satisfy their need to fit in. This easy acceptance creates a misconception in the minds of a number of kids, that just because other kids use drugs with them they are their friends. One student confided how angry, hurt and disappointed he was when he finally figured out that the other kids in his drug abusing group were not really his friends. As long as Mark supplied marijuana or smoked with the group everything was "cool." In reality, other than doing drugs together, these "friends" had nothing in common with Mark and did not care about him as a person. They depended on him to provide his share of pot for the group. This insight sent Mark deeper into abuse. Students told me over and over that **druggies do not make good friends.**

A drug counselor has told me that, in her opinion, each generation has provided less guidance to young people than the one before. She feels we have reached the point where, for many kids, drug abuse is no big deal. I listened to a mother in a support group for parents of abusers say, "It seems like today's parents are a generation of enablers." Every single student in the drug treatment program at our school knows one or more adults they can use with. Some parents make drugs available in their homes. Others do not directly supply the alcohol and marijuana but fail to discourage the kids from using in their homes. **Teenage users know the homes in which they can**

smoke and drink and those in which this behavior will not be tolerated.

When children are raised in homes where family members openly use drugs another problem often develops. Growing up in this environment negates the anti-drug information they receive at school. How are educators to get through to students when the adults in their lives are such poor role models? Mixed messages of this kind will probably result in the children following their parents.

Boredom and too much leisure time are a dangerous combination for teenagers. Young people who lack hobbies and extra-curricular interests will frequently turn to drugs just to give themselves something to do.

Rebellion is a big reason teenagers abuse drugs. I asked the students who offered this reason exactly what they meant. Some teenagers are angry and have developed a strong sense of resentment toward their parents. These kids abuse drugs knowing they will upset their parents. The students say they are angry because their parents do not care about them, do not listen to them, they are over-controlling or they do not spend enough time with their children.

If teenagers can get away with it, some will stay out and socialize all night. Drug abuse is frequently included in these nocturnal get-togethers. Kids do this because they do not like where they live, they are bored, nobody else is at home or they want to be with their boyfriend or girlfriend. Parents should be aware of the experience of a deputy sheriff who says it is not unusual for worried parents to call his office at six or seven o'clock in the morning to report a missing child. The first questions he asks the parent are: where did your child go, and who was he or she with? The deputy sheriff says that an increasing number of parents are unable to answer either question. This lack of parental involvement is a serious warning sign of trouble ahead.

Some kids are trying to develop independence from their smothering parents. Teenagers in this situation want some control over their own lives. They are being taught not to do drugs, but if they are angry enough, these kids will defy their parents. They feel adults are constantly telling them what to do and what not to do. For them, fun begins when they determine the rules and ignore the adults. Drug abuse is something these teenagers do on their own terms; they do not care how upsetting this can be for others.

During the early stages of drug use, usually during middle school, if kids are not caught and forced to suffer negative consequences, the experience can be fun and exciting. All the adult warnings seem inaccurate and unimportant. Risk provides an adrenaline rush, along with the euphoric effects of the drugs. The teenagers know they are doing something illegal, that adults are against it, and if they are caught they will be in trouble. This all adds excitement to the experience.

Curiosity is another reason to experiment with drugs. The media is dangerously effective in stimulating curiosity about drugs for teenagers. Students tell me movies and music are the two worst influences. Kids also hear others talking about taking drugs and describing their effects. When younger kids listen to their role models and friends glorify drug use they are more likely to begin experimenting. Teenagers want to see for themselves what the attraction is all about and how the drugs will make them feel.

Some teenagers take drugs because they really do like the way the drugs make them feel. The sensations these kids experience is what motivates them. While under the influence, it allows a number of adolescents a **temporary** escape from the expectations of the real world. They can forget homework, responsibility, and commitments to others.

We teach students in our classes about the concept of a genetic predisposition for drug addiction. For example, the disease of alcoholism can be inherited. After I explain this process I ask for a show of hands from those who have noticed a pattern of alcoholism in their families passed from generation to generation. For example, let us say your grandma on your father's side, your uncle (father's brother) and your cousin (uncle's daughter) are all alcoholics. In a typical class of thirty students five to ten hands will go up; I have had as many as fifteen. I caution the students who raised their hands that they too could have a genetic link to alcoholism. Students who have noted this pattern in their family must monitor their alcohol consumption closely. Otherwise, they might become the next alcoholic on their family tree. Better yet, they should not drink at all and then the problem never has a chance to start. Most drug experts I have heard speak on this topic agree that the genetic propensity for drug addiction encompasses other drugs of abuse in addition to alcohol. As soon as some kids start using, their addiction begins.

Proactive Advice for Parents

I interviewed a support group for parents who have experienced the ordeal of a son or daughter abusing drugs and they offered some advice to young parents. One of the questions I asked was, "If you could turn back time to when your children were toddlers, knowing what you know now, what would you do differently?" Some parents told me they would not change much at all. A mother said she felt she had done everything within her power to prevent this nightmare, yet in spite of her best efforts her child still abused drugs. There are no guarantees when it comes to parenting. A couple of parents in the group felt they had done a good job but still failed. The following suggestions will not ensure that parents will have drug-free children but, if followed, they should significantly decrease the likelihood of their children developing drug problems.

Drugs know no socio-economic or geographic boundaries. Parents should never feel immune to drug problems in their home. Some parents confessed to me that they noticed warning signs but did nothing. They wonder what might have happened if they had intervened during the early stages of their child's drug use instead of living in denial. They convinced themselves that their child would never do something like that. Parents mentioned finding drug paraphernalia in their child's bedroom, a marijuana plant growing in the back yard, changes in friends, the smell of marijuana on clothing, a drop in grades, and dropping out of extra-curricular activities. The warning signs of drug abuse are well documented in books on the subject. **When parents first become suspicious they must intervene.** Denial will add fuel to a fire that can quickly burn out of control. A mother confided that she was not sure what her son's drug paraphernalia was, so she did nothing. She told me, "Right then and there I should have taken it to someone who could tell me what those objects were." She did nothing and her son's abuse continued and increased, unchecked.

Running a close second to denial is being an enabler. One parent who was going through a difficult divorce said that when her son was doing poorly in school, she would blame the teachers. She would also blame herself for being an ineffective mother. **She never confronted her son and held him accountable for his own actions.** She always covered for him whenever he made bad decisions. This mother now advises parents who find themselves in this situation to, "separate your own feelings from your child's feelings. If your son or daughter makes a poor decision and feels guilty or depressed, you should not feel the same way." Every parent in the support group agreed that when kids make bad decisions parents must not over-compensate by making excuses for their child. One said, "Don't rescue your kid— let him suffer the consequences." Another regretted using too much positive reinforcement. He said he complimented his son when he knew the boy really did not deserve it. A mother chimed in with, "I wish I had said **no** more often."

Part of being an enabler is not expecting children to live within the rules of the family. I was surprised by the number of teenage drug abusers who told me that **kids really do want discipline**. Without structure and guidelines, coupled with negative consequences for bad decisions, kids do not feel their parents care about them.

I also interviewed students who were drug free. I asked them why they made the decision to stay away from drugs. Several mentioned the fear factor. They were afraid of what would happen if their parents discovered they were abusing drugs. One girl said her parents clearly spelled out what the consequences would be if they caught her and went on to say there was no doubt that they would follow through. In her mind, experimenting with drugs, including alcohol was not worth the consequences she would face if her parents found out.

I once heard an expression, **"Rules without relationship equal rebellion."** For lenient parents who have not earned the respect of their children, the fear factor will fail miserably. Part of what the kids are talking about involves the fear of disappointing their parents. The mutual love and respect between a parent and a child, built up over years, will have a positive influence on a teenager's decision-making process. Without this bond the parents who suddenly want to get tough with the discipline of their children will have a rebellion on their hands. Teenagers who could care less if they hurt or anger their parents will not respond positively to a "get tough" approach.

The purpose of discipline is not to punish but to correct. Parents who are enablers fail to teach their children how to make positive choices. **Without structure and guidelines these unfortunate students do not grasp the concept that bad decisions result in negative consequences.** As a result, choosing to use drugs is one more mistake in a long line of bad moves. In most cases law enforcement personnel will eventually become involved and attempt to teach these kids what their parents did not. Establishing discipline within the framework of mutual love and respect must start during the formative years. Parents who try using a new set of strict rules after their teenager develops a drug problem can expect a nightmare.

Parents must understand the importance of the middle school years. This is usually the time students decide whether they will or will not become involved with drugs. The stage is then set for the high school years which is when abuse accelerates. The concept of gateway drugs is well known but unfortunately some parents do not take these warning signs seriously. Experimentation with cigarettes, alcohol and marijuana during middle school should be seen as red flags. Students at my high school have told me, "If kids are smoking cigarettes, it is almost a sure bet they will eventually smoke marijuana," and "Weed starts everything."

Keep the lines of communication open and be willing to spend time listening to your children before you expect them to be receptive to your parental advice. **Teenagers must know you care before they care about what you know.** When parents ask their children how their day went many kids respond with a simple "fine" or "okay." Parents who have trouble getting their children to open up could ask more specific questions:

- What is your toughest subject right now?
- Did anything fun happen today?
- How are your friends doing? How is Angela getting along?
- Who is your favorite teacher this semester? Why?
- (After a big test or project) How did it go? Did you get your grade back yet? Did the teacher say anything to you about it?

Once the kids start talking and realize their parents are really listening, the lines of communication open up and the relationship continues in the right direction.

It is especially important for parents to monitor the friends of their children in grades five through nine. This is, however, a sensitive issue and must be handled carefully. I have heard parents say you cannot pick your children's friends for them. I believe that is true up to a point but **the way in which parents raise their children can influence who they select for their friends.** The values parents instill in their kids affect many of the decisions children make, including their choice of friends. With that said, most parents will probably still notice one or more of their children's friends they would prefer to see excluded from the group.

I found with our kids that, when this happened, the girls eventually figured things out by themselves. My wife and I tried to be respectful toward *any* friend they invited into our home. Parents should be alert for opportunities to ask questions in a non-threatening manner. For example, when you hear your child make a negative statement about a questionable friend, you could ask, "What are some of the qualities about Ellen that made you decide to choose her for a friend?" And possibly, "It does not appear you enjoy yourself when you are with Ellen. Am I wrong when I say that?" At some point during the conversation it might be helpful to review the following qualities of a true friend:

- friends will not intentionally harm you
- friends will support you
- friends will be good listeners whom you can trust
- friends will be there when you need them, and
- friends will multiply your happiness and divide your sorrow.

Parents could follow up these guidelines with, "Do you feel Ellen is a good friend?" Kids are smart and, with some tactful guidance, can usually figure out who is a real friend and who is not. These ideas worked well for our family.

Starting in middle school there will be parties and other social events that teenagers want to attend. Our daughters both told me they knew ahead of time what kind of party it was going to be by finding out **where the party was to be held and who was to be there.** When we were hosting bonfires after the home football games I began to worry when close to one hundred kids started showing up. Even though we had plenty of adult chaperones, drug abuse was still a concern. I discussed this with some of my daughters' friends and they reassured me, "Don't worry, Mr. Gangstad. The kids who smoke and drink don't want to come to a party like this one."

When kids attend a middle school party, or even a high school party, parents should know where the party is being held. This is another touchy area with some teenagers and must be handled carefully. If your son or daughter is going to a party at a home where you do not know the parents, I suggest you learn more. Call the parents who are hosting the party and offer to send snacks or drinks. This is a subtle way to make sure these parents know about the party and, hopefully, will be there as chaperones. Spend a few minutes talking with them and express your gratitude for their hospitality.

It also helps to periodically talk to your kids about drugs. If the subject comes up on television, in a newspaper, a magazine or even songs, take these opportunities to share your feelings. This can be a good topic for a family dinner discussion. More and more teenagers are now, as a drug counselor put it, "Out of reach from their parents." Today, some teenagers' bedrooms are in reality separate living areas with all the amenities: computer (internet), telephone, television, bathroom, stereo, microwave, and refrigerator. These kids can almost lead an existence separate from the rest of their family. **Parents will have a difficult time staying connected to a child they rarely see.** Cell phones, the internet, and easy access to cars make the need to lay the groundwork when the children are young more important than ever before. **Parents should not count on the schools to do their job for them.** Teachers should reinforce the anti-drug message parents begin at home. Based on over three decades of teaching experience I can say that our anti-drug abuse lesson plans will probably fall on deaf ears if the parents have not laid this foundation.

Parents need to be clear in their own minds why they expect their children to say no to drugs. If a teenage boy asks his mother, "What is wrong with smoking some weed with my friends, as long as we are careful?" she needs to know how to respond. If she is not sure of her own feelings on the issue her uncertainty will be conveyed to her son. For example, if the mother answers, "Because it is illegal to smoke marijuana." What will she say when her son then asks, "If weed were legal, would you mind me smoking it?" My point, again, is that kids are smart and they can see through, as well as take advantage of, parental weaknesses. **So, why are you against your kids using drugs?** The answer to that question is the message you must communicate to your children. However, without a trusting and caring relationship in which respect is reciprocal the message may not get through.

The students I interviewed had some good advice for parents. I asked them, "What is wrong with kids experimenting with drugs?" "What is wrong with drinking a few beers at the party on Saturday night?" "What is the big deal about smoking pot over at your friend's house?" The students told me that nobody knows ahead of time who can take drugs in moderation (including alcohol) and still remain in control. Nobody knows ahead of time who can use drugs in a social setting yet not become addicted. In one student's words, "All kids want independence and more control over their own lives. When kids get drunk or high, they lose partial control over their bodies. People do things under the influence that they would never do in a normal situation. Fights, accidents, and offensive comments which can damage relationships often happen as a result of drug abuse." I was reminded of race car driver Al Unser Junior's comment at his press conference before checking into a drug treatment center. Little Al said, "Every bad decision I made over the past few years was directly related to my alcohol abuse." The students I spoke with all agreed that the potential negative effects of getting high were not worth the risk of experiencing the brief euphoria.

For our part, my wife and I said this to each of our two children, "We love you more than our words can possibly express. We have raised you and cared for you since you were a tiny baby. We do not want to see you harmed in any way. If you make the decision to abuse drugs we will be disappointed, hurt, angry, and, most importantly, concerned for your own safety and well-being." I overheard my father-in-law say to some of his grandchildren when they were in elementary school, "If you ever want to kill your poppa you won't need a gun. If any of you kids get involved with drugs and I hear about it that will probably kill me." Our daughters love their grandfather very much and his words made an impression. I repeat, "Rules without relationship equal rebellion."

Learning about drugs will allow parents to communicate more effectively with their children. Videos and books from the public library, parent support groups, law enforcement personnel, AA and NA open meetings are all good sources of information. Parents need to be aware of the different types of drugs, their effects, warning signs, and what drug paraphernalia looks like. Both parents and teenagers should be aware of the laws concerning use and possession. When hosting a party, parents assume certain responsibilities and the legal obligations can add to their own risk. If a teenager gets high at a party held in someone's house and has an accident driving home, a trial lawyer has an easy task proving negligence on the part of the hosts.

Divorce is an issue in many families. The breakup of a marriage can have long-lasting consequences for members of the broken family. It is no coincidence that many of the students and parents who have experienced drug problems have also suffered through a divorce. Some divorced parents offered good advice to others facing this domestic trauma. Parents need to explain to their children that even though the divorce is sad it is permanent. Mom and Dad will not be getting back together. Kids must know that even though their parents do not love each other anymore, they are still loved by their parents. All members of the family should learn from the past, make changes, and move forward with their lives. The divorced parents all agreed that these words are easy to say but, in reality, are tough to follow. However, when parents and children do not effectively deal with a divorce, drug abuse is one of the possible outcomes. Local support groups can be helpful in working through this process.

A single mother told me she believed she should have made a greater effort to find a positive male role model for her son. After her divorce there was a void created by the absence of the boy's father. With hindsight, she wished she had pushed harder for her son's grandfather and uncle to provide more guidance. She said that both men offered their support but she preferred not to bother them at the time. Another divorced mother, with a teenage daughter, expressed similar regrets. With her father no longer around, the young lady did not experience the appropriate way for a man to treat a lady. Without her father's consistent love and support she tried to fill the void in her life with one boyfriend after another. Sexual promiscuity in teenagers often goes hand in hand with drug abuse.

When students are involved in after-school programs it also helps them avoid drug use. I asked an administrator at our school if his own kids, who are all adults now, experienced any drug-related problems as they were growing up. He shook his head no. I followed up with, "Off the top of your head, why do you think your kids avoided drugs?" His immediate response was, **"A heavy involvement in extra-curricular activities."** He mentioned other reasons his kids had stayed away from drugs but I thought his initial response was significant. Students who work hard to succeed in athletics, performing arts and other activities will not be as willing to jeopardize their progress by getting caught with drugs. Dedicated athletes will be less likely to diminish gains achieved through strength and conditioning programs by abusing drugs. The time commitment involved after school also keeps teenagers busy in productive ways, cutting down the amount of free time they have in which to get in trouble.

The friendships which form between participants in extra-curricular activities, friendships that in some cases last a lifetime, can be helpful in assisting the teenagers to remain drug free. Parents attend games and performances to support their children. As the parents sit together, week after week and season after season, they too form friendships. Such friendships make it much easier for parents to network and to monitor what is happening in the lives of their children. In the words of one mother, "I loved that part the most. This togetherness carries down to the children."

I talked with a recovering alcoholic who told me that, as he looked back on his own abuse, he felt he was addicted to alcohol after the first time he got drunk. I remember him saying, "The first time I got drunk was just like the last time I got drunk. I got sick and I got in trouble." He added that many relatives on his father's side of the family were alcoholics. For teenagers with this genetic link to addiction, even experimenting with one gateway drug can lead straight to serious abuse.

"You took drugs when you were young, so why can't I?" This is a reasonable question requiring a reasonable answer. Be honest with your kids. If you used drugs, **do not glorify it** but tell the truth. Teenagers appreciate honesty and they will not respect a hypocrite or a liar. This situation provides another opportunity to reinforce the specific reasons why you are against the experimental and social use of drugs. Drug abuse has always been dangerous but the stakes are now higher than ever before. The marijuana being smoked today has a much higher content of the psychoactive ingredient, THC, than the pot smoked by previous generations. The sale of designer drugs that are produced in home labs has risen dramatically and kids do not know what harmful chemicals they contain. When "picking battles" with your kids, without question, this is one you need to fight and win. Make it clear to your children that if they **choose** to step over the line the consequences will be severe. **This approach must, however, begin in the children's formative years and never**

waiver. This family rule should not be negotiable: *drug abuse will not be tolerated in this home.*

Although teenagers abuse a variety of drugs I want to discuss marijuana because I believe pot is a more serious problem than some people are aware. I have come to agree with the student who told me, "Weed starts everything." A middle school student said, "Marijuana is easier to get and conceal than alcohol." Another teenager told me how he has watched kids he knows smoke weed on a regular basis and end up "losing at life."

As part of our discussion on marijuana I share the following story with my class. It concerns a football player who won the Heisman Trophy. This talented athlete became the number one draft choice for an NFL team in need of a quality running back. He consequently arrived in training camp with high expectations. Surprisingly, his rookie season was a big disappointment. When his second year was also unproductive this former Heisman Trophy winner was cut from the team. During the next season, he was interviewed by ESPN about his attempt to make a comeback with a new team. The commentator asked him what the problem was with his former team. His answer should send a strong message to parents: he confessed that after winning the Heisman Trophy he began smoking pot in increasing amounts. As his abuse grew, his performance on the football field deteriorated. This athlete went on to say that **the negative effects of marijuana came on so gradually he did not notice.** The coaches, players, and fans could see something was wrong, but he failed to do so until it was too late. He concluded that, **"Marijuana made me lazy."** The young man was cut from the new team and I have not heard of him since. As a high school teacher and former coach, I believe marijuana abuse (combined with sleep deprivation and poor nutrition) helps cause the apathy I see in so many of our students.

Drug experts refer to this as the Amotivational Syndrome. From daily observations at my high school I am convinced the syndrome is real.

As our class discussion on marijuana continues, I ask my students to think of people they know who frequently smoke pot. I inquire whether they have noticed worrisome symptoms in those people that in their opinion are **directly related to their marijuana abuse.** I write their observations on the board in front of the class. By the end of the period the students have usually compiled a lengthy list which, typically, includes the following: memory loss, moodiness, depression, laziness, falling grades, change of friends, dropping out of extra-curricular activities, trouble at school, family problems, being arrested, boredom, change in appearance, more frequent illness, progression to other drugs (gateway concept), failure to set goals for the future, weight gain, and stealing. When the students finish, I ask them to carefully look over ***their*** list. Then, I add a few more concerns they failed to mention.

At our school we have an excellent, informative video tape in which drug expert David L. Ohlms, MD, presents a lecture on marijuana. Dr. Ohlms supports many of the observations the students themselves make and he adds further concerns based on his research. For example, Dr Ohlms notes that marijuana can cause oral cancer, it has twice as many carcinogens as tobacco. He also states that marijuana is addictive. When a person stops smoking pot he or she does not immediately go into withdrawal because it takes weeks for the THC stored in the body's fatty tissues to leave the body. The brain, ovaries, and testicles are made up in part of fatty tissue. Detoxification of marijuana is not like going "cold turkey" with alcohol. Alcohol is water soluble and if not replenished leaves the body much quicker than marijuana. The THC in marijuana is fat soluble and dissipates more slowly. That is how drug tests can detect the presence of THC three to four weeks after the individual has smoked a joint. There is no doubt the influence of marijuana can be a factor in causing accidents.

We close our discussion by considering the following question: "Based on what you have heard today, can you honestly say marijuana should be decriminalized or even legalized?" Unfortunately, this lesson has no visible effect on some of my students. Denial is a common defense mechanism among drug abusers including those who smoke marijuana. Do not allow yourself to be one of the parents who must admit, **"I had no idea."** In conclusion, parents must do all they can to avoid the living hell that results from a child involved with drug abuse.

Notes for Chapter Nine
Drugs

Notes for Chapter Nine
Drugs

The Awkward Years

Chapter Ten
Elementary School to Middle School

My younger daughter rolls her eyes when she thinks back to the time she refers to as the awkward years. Both girls cringe whenever they look at pictures of themselves during this phase of their lives. I know I have looked at some old pictures of myself at that age and thought, "What in the world was I thinking?" Puberty is the time when children's bodies transform into those of young adults. While kids are dealing with menstrual cycles, braces, cracking voices and the challenge of shaving for the first time, they are trying to determine who they are and where they fit in the grand scheme of things.

Compounding this identity crisis is the realization that middle school life is largely centered on material issues. What are the right clothes to wear? Who is in the popular group and how can I gain entry? What is the cool way to act? Middle school exposes kids to many more experiences than before, both good and bad. For many students, parties or informal gatherings at someone's house mean more than just pizza, soft drinks and renting a movie. An invitation or lack thereof to a middle school social event can boost or diminish an adolescent's self-esteem. Some students consider inclusion in the social circle of the popular group a major accomplishment. Compared to elementary school, there are plenty of extra-curricular activities. The activities students select can influence the way they are perceived by their classmates. Students frequently form cliques at this time.

Parents become concerned when students begin to make adult-like decisions on their own. This is when parents are no longer at their children's sides telling them what to do, a time when peer pressure is at its strongest. Adolescents are faced with choices concerning alcohol, drugs, and sex. Many believe they are old enough to handle themselves and these issues when, in reality, they are just getting started in life. Parents should give their kids sufficient freedom to make minor mistakes, but not enough to enable them to make mistakes with long-term consequences. Parents should be involved in their children's lives to the point where they know what is going on, but not be so overly involved that they try to relive their own childhood through their children. At this time, more than ever before, we must **be a parent, not a friend to our children.** That does not, of course, mean you should not be a friendly parent.

My first seven years in teaching were at the middle school level and I call upon the insights from those times, along with my experience helping raise two daughters, to support my advice. In this chapter I will discuss the following points:

- friends and cliques
- clothes
- gossip
- staying connected to your middle school child
- tough times for self-esteem
- money
- overindulgence
- picking your battles wisely
- sex education
- sports
- responsibility, and
- dealing with a teacher your child does not like.

The start of middle school is a significant time for children. Having good friends is going to be an important part of a positive school experience. However, several factors can complicate friendships. Unless you are in a small community, several elementary schools will be sending sixth graders to your child's middle school. The security of neighborhood and elementary school friendships can be threatened as old friends start to expand their circle to include new faces from other schools. Although cliques take root in fourth and fifth grade, they blossom in middle school. Cliques can be both a good and bad development. For many students the ultimate clique is the popular group. This group consists of the best looking girls and boys, the top athletes/cheerleaders, the kids who wear all the right brand-name clothes and the students closely associated with these people. You will notice that I have not mentioned anything about what the kids in this group are like as people. Many students are not concerned with this most important consideration because the popular group reflects the overemphasis on material issues by middle school adolescents. Some of the kids in the popular group are quality people who would make good friends, but many have their priorities out of order.

Middle school students sometimes make decisions calculated to improve their chances of being included in the popular group. Others intentionally achieve lower grades or only wear clothing with the right brand-name to avoid being looked upon as nerds. Some choose extra-curricular activities based on how they think they will be perceived by their association. Some will succumb to peer pressure in their dealings with sex and drugs in order to be accepted. Social status is also a factor in selecting potential boyfriends/girlfriends. Because of the shallow decision-making process and the low maturity level of middle school students these relationships rarely last more than a few weeks.

Parents observing this process can be a stabilizing influence. First and foremost, as I have said before, be a good listener. Put yourself in the shoes of a middle school student. My wife and I consistently emphasized the importance of character and personality over material considerations. Whenever our kids started new friendships we first asked, "What are they like as people?" We advised our girls that the most important quality in a friend is a good heart. Does he or she live by the Golden Rule? If someone does not have a good heart, then he or she probably will not be a good friend. When parents see their children being hurt by doubtful friends they need to let the kids work out the issues among themselves.

I can remember a time when our younger daughter believed she would be invited to a party given by the popular group. After she discovered she was not on the invitation list I overheard her crying in her room. I then borrowed some wisdom from a newspaper article written by Suzanne Fields. The editorial was titled "The Legacy from Being Daddy's Little Girl." Ms. Fields related her father's words to her in a similar situation when she was growing up.

> "I know you're afraid you won't get accepted. How you see yourself is what counts. You've got to believe in yourself. If you get accepted, that's fine, but if you don't it says nothing about you, only that those girls are unable to know what's good when they see it."

A family moved into our community from another state. One of the daughters began having trouble with some new friends and her parents decided to intervene. The daughter was upset about the way she was being treated by some of the kids in the popular group. The students were picking on her, avoiding her, and excluding her from their activities. Almost every day the girl would come home from school in tears. Finally, the mother decided she was not going to tolerate this behavior any longer. She called the parents of her daughter's questionable friends and let them know she did not appreciate the way in which her daughter was being treated. She expected the parents to talk with their kids and put a stop to the mean-spirited treatment of her daughter. This decision backfired. The mother should have been a good listener, advised her daughter about the characteristics of a true friend, and then allowed her daughter to handle the situation. Instead, the telephone call made the situation worse because it provoked the other girls into excluding her daughter completely.

As an older teenager said when reflecting back on middle school, "I was trying to figure out where I fit in. You don't want to be with the nerds. You want to be with the popular group. But when you really get to know the popular kids, you realize many of them aren't what you thought they would be. At first, it's hard to admit that the nerds are nice, but they are. **You learn that it is better to have many friends from different groups than a few friends from just one group**." This lesson is most effectively absorbed when parents allow their children to learn it on their own.

Clothing is very important to middle school students and, while parents should not underestimate its significance, they need to guide their children to keep the issue in proper perspective. They should stress to them that students wearing expensive brand-name clothes has nothing to do with the kind of a people they are. With that said, I believe it is also a mistake for parents to pass judgment and say, "I think it's ridiculous for these parents to be spending all that money on a shirt just because it has a certain logo. I told my kids there was no way we would waste our money like that and they better not even ask for clothes so over-priced." I think there is a better alternative to this hard line approach. Buy your children the clothes they need. When birthdays and other holidays come around, if they want expensive brand-name clothes for their gifts, even though you may not agree, compromise and buy them what they want. When your kids need additional clothing during the year and if they put the pressure on for high-end clothes, work out a deal. For example, your son wants a shirt from a particular store. It costs $50. At another store, a similar shirt costs $30. In order for both you and your son to be satisfied, contribute the $30 you would have paid at the less expensive store and have your child make up the $20 difference for the shirt of his choice. In this way parents will find out how much their kids really want the expensive clothes and also avoid a possible confrontation. Kids start learning the value of money and may eventually decide that purchasing the lower-priced shirt is a wiser decision.

Gossip runs rampant in middle school. If parents can guide their children in handling this potential powder keg, another source of stress is relieved. Talk to your kids about the whole process and how it works. Tell them not to be gullible and believe everything they hear. Misinformation travels fast in schools. An example occurred one day in a first period weight training class. A student became nauseated and vomited next to the leg press machine. The story was told over and over throughout the school day. At the start of my last period class a student came up to me and said, "We heard a kid had his head crushed in the leg press machine and part of his brains fell out onto the floor."

We advised our daughters that, **"What you do not see with your eyes, do not witness with your mouth."** When students start rumors, or make derogatory comments about other students, word will get back to them and cause trouble. I have seen many fights start over "he said/she said" situations. Learning to handle gossip is important at this level. Students should be told to **try not to say anything behind someone's back that they would not be willing to say to their face or have repeated to that person.**

Parents and their middle school children can begin to drift apart unless the parents make an effort to stay connected. The parents' overall social life should include the school activities in which their children are involved. Getting to know the parents of your children's friends is helpful and socializing with them occasionally is also a good idea. I could sense our kids were pleased when they saw my wife and me enjoying time with the parents of their friends.

However, kids need space away from adults. I have seen some parents take their involvement to the extreme and appear to be trying to relive their own youth through their children and their children's friends. One father comes to mind. He knew as much about what was going on in the students' lives as the kids. Children do not appreciate mothers and fathers hanging around all the time, snooping into their business. I have often wanted to say to such immature adults, "You have had your chance at the good old days. Stay out of the kids' way and let them have their chance." Be supportive from a distance and allow some privacy.

I believe that allowing children to have television sets in their bedrooms contributes to a breakdown in communications by isolating the kids from the rest of the family. Children are more likely to stay in their rooms, with the door closed, watching their own TVs. When kids want to watch TV they can do so with other family members. I can remember many times coming into our bedroom and finding one or both of our daughters on our bed watching our TV. We would turn off the television and start a conversation about their day or I would lie down and view the program with my kids.

Make the evening meal together a priority or the family dinner will slowly disappear and so will wonderful opportunities to stay connected. During family dinners my wife and I liked to give our daughters input on some family decisions. Whenever possible include your children in the life of the family and give them a say in its planning and decisions. When our older daughter was frustrated over various issues in her life she announced that we needed a Family Meeting. I could usually tell by her expression and tone of voice that something was bothering her and she wanted the undivided attention of the entire family. We would all sit down together, not answer the telephone, turn off the TV, and listen as she told us what was bothering her. Sometimes we agreed with her viewpoint and sometimes we did not, but everyone had an opportunity to speak and stay connected with each other.

Middle school can be a tough time on children's self-esteem. Puberty causes major changes in their bodies which may result in an intense, self-conscious concentration on personal appearance. The physical metamorphosis occurs at the same time as appearance assumes a top priority for many students. Some kids take sadistic delight in drawing attention to the more unattractive changes in their classmates. Their mean comments can be hard on an adolescent's self-esteem that is already vulnerable.

Kids are also dealing with social changes that have progressed since the end of their elementary school years. They may start comparing themselves with other students and feel insecure. You can tell your middle school student that excessive comparisons with others could lead to frustration or conceit. There will usually be those who are better and worse, in most respects, than you are. **Be the best you can be.** No matter where kids look they will probably see someone more popular, better dressed, funnier, wealthier, more athletic, more talented, better looking, and smarter than they are. All children are good at something and parents should guide their kids into activities that accentuate *their* interests and strengths. Children need to know they are special and unique and should try not worry about the other kids. Take as much pressure off your children as possible by encouraging them to do the best they can. Who can ask for more?

In one of my classes, I ask my students to respond to this quote from Zig Siglar. "Our problem is that we make the mistake of comparing ourselves with other people. You do not determine your success by comparing yourself to others, rather you determine your success by comparing your accomplishments with your abilities. Do the best you can with what you have, every day." My students relate well to this statement.

Envy is the enemy of happiness and the cause is often money. This lesson is important for middle school students because during this period they are generally more materialistic than ever before. By their example, **parents should demonstrate that success and self-esteem should not be based on how much money people possess.**

Our daughters learned this lesson while babysitting for wealthy families. Sometimes they worked for well-to-do, happy families who had great kids. The parents were easy to work for and appreciated having reliable babysitters. On other occasions our daughters would tell sad stories about poor little rich kids whose parents were too busy to spend time with their lonely and obnoxious children. The parents were difficult to work for which accounted in part for the bad behavior of their children. Our girls would get angry at the way some of the mothers treated them. The ladies were rude, not only to our daughters, but to their own children. To our girls their lives appeared miserable. Sarah and Betsy learned that living in big houses, driving expensive cars and going to fancy country clubs is not always as glamorous or exciting as it appeared to be. They learned that what people are like on the inside is more important than the things they have. Most important, they learned that **self-worth is based on**

strength of character, not material possessions. This insight proved valuable for them as they progressed through the awkward years while living a middle-class existence in an affluent community.

Money is an issue parents must resolve. Should they give kids an allowance? If the answer is yes, how much should be allowed? If the answer is no, where will kids get the money they need? Who establishes priorities when money gets tight and balancing the family budget forces some tough choices? I once listened to a radio talk show discussing the topic of divorce where the studio guest asked, "What is the number one cause of divorce?" I guessed infidelity. The correct answer was disagreements over money. The middle school years can intensify this potential stressor because as kids get older, their activities get more expensive. For wealthy families this is not an issue, but the rest of us must work out **a realistic approach that involves all family members.**

Bills must be paid. Money must be invested for secure retirements. We want comfortable homes, nice cars, and family vacations. Focusing on these responsibilities and desires causes some parents to lose sight of the fact that happiness is found along the way and not at the end of the road. They complain and worry about money to the point that they have trouble finding happiness in their lives and their anxiety can carry over to their children. And when they accumulate money and security, relaxing becomes difficult as they try to dust the cobwebs off their wallets. I realize there are several different ways to effectively deal with this challenge. I would like to share a few tips that worked well in our family.

We embraced the **our money** concept. Any money my wife or I made went into one account. We set our priorities and made decisions together. We had some loud discussions at times but were usually able to work out our differences and compromise. Our kids were aware we were doing okay but sensed, correctly, that there was not a large sum of cash sitting in the bank just waiting to be spent. The girls could see how hard my wife and I were working to provide a good life for them. We decided against giving allowances once a week. We discussed our expectations concerning the work our daughters should do around the house. Sarah and Betsy were a big help and we appreciated their assistance. We tried to develop in our daughters' minds the feeling that, within reason, we would do anything we could for them. We would do this as long as they cooperated and maintained good attitudes towards their chores. Overall, the kids did a good job and when they came to my wife or me asking for money to go to a movie, buy a birthday present for a friend, tickets for a dance, play or concert, we would usually give them what they needed. We believed the girls worked hard for our family and they had earned the money. Remember, we looked at home finances as our money and we all had a sense of ownership.

My wife and I never felt that the girls tried to take advantage of the situation. They knew we were not wealthy and kept their requests to a reasonable level. When possible we tried to be generous with them on our limited funds. Our girls could sense this and I believe they appreciated it. Whenever one of them came to me after an activity to return leftover money I would usually say, "Keep the change; it's a bonus for being a great daughter." When they were old enough to start babysitting we set up their own savings accounts at the bank. We explained how earning money from interest worked. The girls learned to save and still have some fun with their money. Parents must teach their children that no one should spend every dollar they earn. Both girls took pride in earning their own cash instead of always coming to us. Here is another opportunity to use positive eavesdropping. Occasionally, my wife and I would discuss how proud we were of the way they were handling their early earnings. We did this when we knew they could overhear our conversation. While you are talking on the telephone to grandparents and they ask about the kids, tell them the same good news. **Your children will listen when they hear their names mentioned** and this will reinforce what you are trying to teach.

Overindulging children, however, is a pitfall to be avoided. Well-intentioned parents who give their children everything they want will probably experience problems down the line. Their kids do not have to work for anything because they know their parents will give it to them and the value of money becomes difficult to comprehend. I have seen kids such as these lose jackets, shoes, wallets, jewelry, purses, and other costly items, yet never worry for a second. They know their parents will quickly replace lost articles. Instant gratification is the rule of thumb for these kids, because when they want something they get it.

Our older daughter was in second grade when she lost her watch that had been a present from her grandma. Sarah and her mother looked all over but could not find the missing watch. As the search dragged on Sarah became frustrated and said, "Let's just go buy another one. What's the big deal?" Our daughter later told me that my wife responded to her question with words that she remembers to this day. "Don't you understand how many hours your Grandma worked so she could earn the money to buy you that watch?" Teach your children the value of money as soon as they are old enough to comprehend.

Andrew Mullins made a relevant point in his article titled "Classic Fathers," which appeared in *The Weekend Australian.* He said, "Spoiled children will not easily seek happiness in virtue but rather Nintendo and McDonald's. If young children are taught to wait, they will end up less prone to impulsive decisions, less likely to be ruled by their passions and more likely to discover the happiness in life that comes from delaying gratification." When kids are given everything they want they do not understand the concept of appreciation. As they grow older and acquire credit cards, the financial nightmares they create should come as no surprise.

Parents must, however, keep family finances in proper perspective, as the following story illustrates.

> A father punished his five year old daughter for wasting a roll of expensive wrapping paper. Money was tight and he became even more upset when the child pasted the gold paper so as to decorate a box to put under the Christmas tree. Nevertheless, the little girl brought the gift box to her father the next morning and said, "This is for you Daddy." The father was embarrassed by his earlier reaction, but his anger flared again when he found the box was empty. He spoke to her in a harsh manner, "Don't you know, young lady, when you give someone a present there's supposed to be something inside the package?" The little girl looked up at him with tears in her eyes and said, "Oh, Daddy, it's not empty. I blew kisses into it until it was full." The father was crushed. He fell on his knees and put his arms around his little girl; he begged her to forgive him for his unnecessary anger. An accident took the life of the child only a short time later and it is told that the father kept that gold box by his bed for all the years of his life. Whenever he was discouraged or faced difficult problems, he would open the box, take out an imaginary kiss and remember the love of the child who had put it there. In a very real sense, each of us as parents

has been given a golden box filled with unconditional love and kisses from our children. There is no more precious possession anyone could hold.

Although money is important, it should not be the top family priority. Expressing condolences for a child's death is one of the saddest experiences I have ever endured. Over the years I have had to do this on numerous occasions. As I embraced one of my friends I will always remember what he whispered in my ear. Choking back tears he said, "Hug your girls, appreciate them, and tell them you love them every day because none of us knows what tomorrow will bring." It was great advice and should be kept in mind by parents as they decide their approach to family finances. Remember what is most important in life. My father-in-law is the most generous person I have ever known; he is also one the happiest. Although he has limited finances, he is generous with his time, energy, and support. I have come to believe that happiness has a lot more to do with generosity and kindness than with how much money people possess. One of my favorite sayings is, "I don't want to be the richest man in the cemetery."

Part of wisdom lies in knowing what to overlook. Remember the importance of creating a proper balance between being too strict and too lenient. The middle school years will put this balance to the test and the challenge will continue through high school. After progressing through the elementary school years without too many problems parents may suddenly start disapproving of hairstyles, clothing, friends, music, nutrition, sleep patterns, activities, body piercing, tattoos, grades and many other issues that grate on them like sandpaper. **Parents who attempt to micro-mange their children's lives are making a big mistake.** They raise kids who rebel simply trying to elicit a negative reaction from their parents. If they do not rebel, they can grow into dependent young adults who have trouble making it on their own.

Consider these examples of what to overlook. I was concerned our older daughter was not getting enough sleep during the school week. I periodically made comments about her looking tired; each time I did so she bristled. When Sarah began giving me her "don't bug me" look I assured her I was only worried because I loved her, but I could tell she was not impressed by my fatherly instincts. Finally she had had enough and one day when I started in on her she respectfully interrupted and asked, "Dad, are you unhappy with my grades?" I shook my head. Her grades had always been excellent. She continued, "Have I been late or absent from school?" Again, I shook my head. Her attendance record was good. She concluded, "Then why are you bugging me about not getting enough sleep? If my grades drop or I'm missing school, then you have a right to nag me and I'll listen. Until that happens, will you please drop it?" I sat there for a moment, thinking about what she said, as her eyes bored into me. I could not help smiling at her and agreed to drop the subject. I would still have liked to see her get more sleep but decided it was better for natural consequences to be the guide.

Our younger daughter, Betsy, is definitely not the neatest person in the world. I went into her bedroom one day and it really did look like a bomb had blown up in there. My wife had also been reminding her to clean up her room. As the weeks went by the tension increased each time the subject of her messy room was raised. The disagreements reached a point where something had to be done; my wife and I were not going to tolerate the situation any longer. Betsy argued that her bedroom was her personal space and if we did not like the way it looked we should just shut the door so we did not have to see her mess. We agreed that she had a right to her privacy but made sure she understood this was our house. We could have forced her to pick up the mess in her room every day, but once again, this was not a battle we wanted to fight. We worked out a compromise. On Saturday she would pick up the mess in her room, put clean sheets on her bed, dust, and run the vacuum. The rest of the week we would close her door if we did not want to see her clutter. This satisfied both sides and even had a side benefit. As the months and years went by she began to like her Saturday room best and very slowly the messes improved during the week.

Chores can be a trouble spot for parents. I remember directing our girls to do jobs around the house and when they were not completed in what I thought was a reasonable time I started getting upset. The girls had a creative list of excuses. I am an emotional person and freely concede that patience has never been one of my virtues. I could have stood over the kids and forced them to promptly do what I asked but, again, this was not one of the battles I would choose to fight. So, when I had a job for them to do, I asked them to choose a reasonable amount of time for them to complete the work and then expected them to meet that objective. The girls appreciated this approach and our compromise was effective. If parents do not have a good reason for the chores to be completed right away, why expect the children to do them immediately? Allow the kids some flexibility so they can work the requests into their own schedules. We found that when we occasionally needed their help right that instant, they understood and willingly helped out. Wise parents will learn to overlook, compromise and, only when necessary, take a stand.

Although sex education is a topic many parents prefer not to think about, they should understand that middle school is a time of runaway hormones. When I became a father for the first time I was looking for advice on how to be a good parent. An older friend of ours had a good relationship with his four teenage children so I asked him for suggestions. He gave me a good one regarding the birds and the bees: he believed the father should explain sexuality and reproduction to the daughters and the mother should do so for the sons. After the initial explanations both parents can work together as appropriate. Our friend believed this approach brought him closer to his girls at a time when staying connected was becoming more of a challenge. Years later I followed his advice and we survived this milestone.

Share true stories and examples with your children whenever they relate to skills for living. Teen pregnancy was a topic that afforded me this effective approach to teaching life lessons. I told our girls about a young lady in my class who was about two or three months pregnant. The girl was having morning sickness almost every day and was issued a permanent pass by the health center so that each time she felt nauseated she could excuse herself from class and hurry to the restroom. She was doing the best she could but was still having a tough time keeping up with her studies. Within a few more weeks she dropped out of school, lost her credits for that semester, and I never saw her again. After years in public education I had many such stories to tell our daughters about the difficulties associated with teenage pregnancy. All parents need to look for real-life examples for their kids to learn from.

An all-day babysitting job taught our girls the most powerful lesson. A couple was going to the Indy 500 with friends from out of town. Our middle-school-age daughters were excited to be paid double to stay with the young children from both families. After the race the adults were going to a party and planned to return home around ten o'clock. Our girls started at seven in the morning and came home, exhausted, at ten-thirty that evening. They both earned a good amount of money but said they would never take on such a job again. They learned that taking care of young children all day is hard work. After listening to the girls' version of how the day went, I smiled as I heard them say, "I'm not having any kids for a *long* time." This experience may have had as much impact on them as anything I had to say about unplanned pregnancies.

From my observation, many sexually promiscuous girls have had either a terrible relationship with their father or no father in their home. Either way, the absence of a father's love has left an emotional void in their lives. These deprived girls are deluded into thinking that having sex is the same thing as making love. As they go from boy to boy they become emptier and lonelier as they fail to find the missing element in their lives. Unfortunately, as more boys use and abuse them, more hardships start to develop, such as sexually transmitted diseases, unplanned pregnancies and tarnished reputations. Additional emotional problems surface as they begin to understand what they are doing to themselves. This is a further quote from Suzanne Field's editorial titled, "The Legacy of Being Daddy's Little Girl":

> "For many women life with father is a dress rehearsal for love and marriage. How a young girl is treated by her father can determine what she will expect from men in her life. We hear a lot about the increasing number of boys who are deprived of a role model because there's no father at home to imitate. Girls without fathers suffer a different kind of loss. Girls get a glimpse of the woman blossoming inside themselves when they have a loving father."

Many of my students do not understand the difference between love and infatuation. At some point, middle school parents need to include this topic in their sex education discussions. Over the years, kids in my classes have related effectively to the following lesson. For parents who are a little uncomfortable with this topic, these diagrams may be helpful in opening up the lines of communication.

I draw the following two figures on the board. I ask which one represents love and which figure symbolizes infatuation. They need to explain the significance of the numbers as well as the different positions of the two triangles. I ask them to give some real-life examples to support their viewpoint. This is a meaningful experience for the students who never seriously thought about this topic before.

Love or Infatuation?

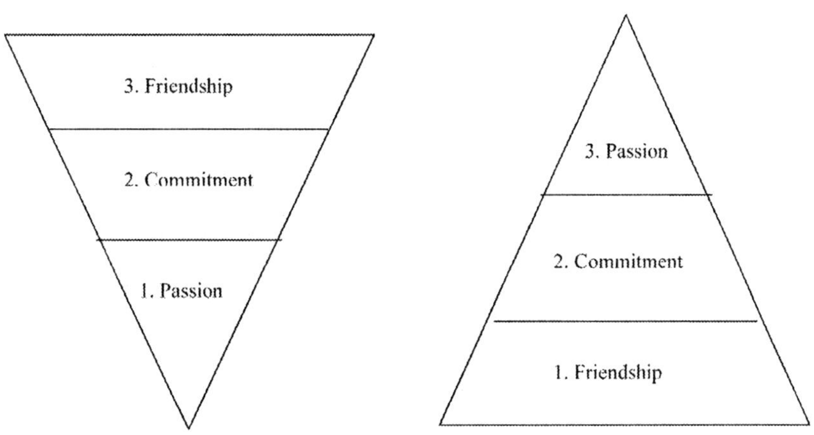

Participation in middle school sports will require support and guidance from parents. I would like to offer a few suggestions for parents whose children are interested in athletics. As young athletes progress from grade school to middle school, *if there is an interest*, parents should encourage their children to play a different sport in the fall, winter, and spring seasons. Specializing in one sport at a young age can be a mistake. Playing different sports is not only fun, but it provides some variety in their routines. If kids are not given an opportunity to try different activities, how will they know their true strengths? For parents of young kids interested in athletics remember the important message from *The Ugly Duckling.* I have witnessed the transformation of clumsy middle school kids into talented high school seniors who earn athletic scholarships. I have also seen outstanding middle school athletes passed up by the time they reached high school because they matured early, lost interest or failed to keep training properly. At the middle school level parents should stay positive and encourage their children's interests. Many surprising changes can and do occur between sixth grade and high school.

John Shaughnessy wrote an excellent newspaper editorial titled, "Organized Play Threatens to Devalue Joy of Childhood." He said:

> "The focus of childhood play has long turned away from delightfully unstructured mostly unsupervised games centralized in the neighborhood. Sandlots are empty while children fill sports camps often costing hundreds of dollars for a few days. Knocks at the door to invite a friend to play are greeted by announcements that the child is at a lesson. All-star teams that once traveled across the city for competition now tour the state, the country. Even worse, that emphasis begins earlier and earlier for children."

Although this change is hard for some parents to accept, children interested in athletics need to be guided through the reality of today. Focusing on the good old days is counter-productive for kids living in the twenty-first century.

In his article "Having Fun Is What Sports Are All About," Rick Wolff wrote:

> "More and more these days, dismayed parents of junior and senior high athletes tell me they've become disappointed when their youngsters, who have played competitive sports since age six, say they're no longer interested in committing themselves to play on high school varsity teams. A simple case of burnout? Perhaps. As our children take up competitive sports at early ages, and then become fully immersed with travel, select, elite, or premier squads, we really shouldn't be surprised when a youngster begins to differentiate between playing one sport "for fun" and another "because I'm supposed to work at it."

Indianapolis has a semi-pro football team. In the sports section of our newspaper there appeared a feature article about one of the young men who plays the position of tight end. He is in his early twenties, 6'5" tall, and weighs 260 pounds. The coach says he catches passes from the quarterback as well as any receiver he has ever seen. This young man always wanted to play football, but until this year, he had never done so. In the article he told his story and expressed his regret that he had specialized in basketball. From little league through college he focused all his spare energy on this one sport. In high school, as he started to mature, his interest in football was discouraged because he was told it might interfere with his chances of earning a basketball scholarship.

He did earn a scholarship to a small college and had a mediocre basketball experience, but at the rate he is improving on the semi-pro football team, the coach believes an NFL tryout is a real possibility. This young man has a message for students interested in athletics. He advises kids to keep their options open and, if interested, play more than one sport. He wonders how his life might have been different had he played both sports in middle school and high school.

Parents must teach their children to be responsible. **The best way to instill this important value is to give them responsibilities and then hold them accountable.** When our children were in the transition years between elementary school and middle school my wife and I could sense they were ready to take on more responsibilities. We saw an opportunity to accommodate this through babysitting. When our older daughter was in sixth grade we made a proposal to both of our girls, giving them a "responsibility test." The girls would stay home by themselves and if they demonstrated they were capable of handling the situation, we would pay each of them instead of paying our regular babysitter. Neither girl would be in charge. They would both work together. The girls were enthusiastic and quickly agreed to our proposal. As my wife and I walked out the door for dinner and a movie we reminded the girls that this was an experiment and, if they did well, we would give them more chances in the future. If they were negligent, we would need to bring back our old babysitter and pay her. Our girls loved this arrangement and did a good job. We were proud and we told them so. Within a year our older daughter began babysitting for the children of other families. In a few more years her younger sister followed in her footsteps. When children demonstrate irresponsible behavior, it becomes more difficult for parents to have confidence in their kids. I feel bad for the growing number of parents who cannot trust their own children. **Trust must be earned and this is an ongoing process.**

The daily schedule of middle school students includes five, six and possibly seven different teachers. This is significantly different from many elementary school routines. Occasionally, they will get a teacher they do not like. As in any profession teaching has a few weak links in the educational chain. Parents should seek out the specific reasons why their child does not like a particular teacher. Usually, problems originate from a personality conflict. In these cases the child needs to learn how to get along and adapt in ways that will allow him or her to make it through the class. Students are not required to like their teachers; but they do need to demonstrate respect. Who hasn't had a boss they did not like? In life we all must learn to be flexible, adjust, and still get the job done. Parents should tell students this is a good way to prepare for the real world. When they later find themselves under a boss they dislike, the young adults will be forced to use many of the same coping skills learned back in the classroom with those dreaded teachers.

Occasionally, problems with a teacher are more serious than a personality conflict. As parents listen to their children and identify the issues, they should offer suggestions to see if the student can work things out with the teacher. If the trouble persists after several weeks and is having a negative effect on learning, parents need to call the teacher and get involved. After communicating with the teacher, if the situation does not improve, then parents should take their concern to the next administrative level.

For some students middle school will come and go without too many complications. For many others there will be bumps, potholes, and wrong turns on the road to high school. As children leave behind the security of elementary school, parents can ease the stress of the awkward years by providing guidance and support. Remember to keep the big picture in mind as you deal with all these issues. Appreciate each phase of your children's lives and help them do the same. As John Madden points out in his book, *One Size Doesn't Fit All:*

> "I've always believed in doing two things with kids.
> One is getting them to enjoy what they're doing now;

the other is encouraging them, but not rushing them. From the time children are born until they graduate from college, adults are always rushing them into the future. By that time, some kids have been so busy worrying about where they're going that they never had time to enjoy where they've been."

Notes for Chapter Ten
Elementary School to Middle School

When I was fourteen years old, my parents were so ignorant I could hardly stand to have them around. By the time I was twenty-one, I was amazed by how much they had learned in seven years.

~ Mark Twain

Chapter Eleven
Middle School to High School

For many parents the high school commencement ceremony is accompanied by mixed emotions as family and friends reflect back on four years that seemed to pass by all too quickly. For others those years seem more like a nightmare. Errors of judgment, made with the best of intentions, leave some parents feeling guilty, angry, frustrated, embarrassed, disappointed, and, in some cases, heartbroken.

In this chapter I will discuss the following points:

- trust, but verify
- four keys to raising children who will enjoy high school
- easing the transition from middle school to high school
- relate to your kids in such a way that you have few regrets when they leave home
- remember, you are making memories
- creating an inviting home for your children and their friends
- changing friendships – do not burn your bridges
- dating issues
- summer and part-time jobs
- cars, and
- preparing for life after high school.

Children in high school present parents with a new unique set of challenges. Today's parents need to develop some street smarts in order to keep up with their kids; occasionally they may even need to outwit them. **Kids need to understand that although their parents may have been born at night, they were not born *last* night.** The following story illustrates my point.

Jim invited his mother over for dinner. During the course of the meal, Jim's mother couldn't help but notice how beautiful Jim's roommate, Stephanie, was. Mrs. Gregory had long been suspicious of a relationship between Jim and his roommate, and this had only made her more curious. Over the course of the evening, while watching the two, Mrs. Gregory started to wonder if there was more between Jim and Stephanie than met the eye. Reading his Mom's thoughts, Jim volunteered, "I know what you must be thinking, but I assure you Stephanie and I are just roommates." About a week later, Stephanie came to Jim saying, "Ever since your mother came to dinner, I've been unable to find the beautiful silver gravy ladle. You don't suppose she took it do you?" Jim said, "Well, I doubt it, but I'll send her an e-mail just to be sure." So he sat down and wrote,

Dear Mother,

I'm not saying that you 'did' take the gravy ladle from the house, and I'm not saying that you 'did not' take the gravy ladle. But the fact remains that one has been missing ever since you were here for dinner.

Love, Jim

Several days later, Jim received a reply from his mother that read,

Dear Son,

I'm not saying that you 'do' sleep with Stephanie, and I'm not saying that you 'do not' sleep with Stephanie. But the fact remains that if she were sleeping in her own bed, she would have found the gravy ladle by now.

Love, Mom

Although parents should trust their children, they still need to know what is going on in their lives. President Reagan was involved in a nuclear arms summit with the Soviet Union. He had developed a good working relationship with the Russian premier, Mikhail Gorbachev. One of the issues they were discussing was accountability for arms reduction. During a news conference one of the reporters asked whether, in the light of the improved relations between the two superpowers, they could not just trust each other to do what was agreed upon at the summit? Ronald Reagan responded to the journalist with a couple of diplomatic comments but finished with the words: **trust, but verify.** This advice is as good for parents dealing with their children as it is for superpowers. Respect your high school children's privacy but be aware of what is happening in their lives so you can be proactive in dealing with the issues that surface.

The children who attend smaller high schools may face minimal transition problems. After talking with students, teachers, and coaches from both small and large high schools I believe there are advantages and disadvantages to both situations. All of my experience as a student, teacher, and parent, has been with large high schools. I know many parents worry that their children will get lost in the shuffle and be overwhelmed in a large school. They believe their kids will not get the attention they need from teachers and counselors or that they will not be able to compete with so many athletes, musicians, performers, and academically gifted students. Parents are worried by the perceived presence of bad kids in public schools. Some hope that by enrolling their children in a private school they will avoid exposure to drugs and thugs. I can understand these concerns but I believe such worries can be alleviated with proper guidance and effective parenting.

I am an advocate for public education. At the public school where I teach we are experiencing a growing number of students who transfer back from neighboring private schools. When I ask these kids why they returned they give some answers that parents might find interesting. According to these children and much to their parents' surprise, drug abuse at the private schools is as bad as, if not worse than, that found in public schools. In most cases our facilities are superior. Since we a have a much larger school we are able to offer a much broader curriculum. Although we have over three thousand students, returnees tell me they receive plenty of attention and that our faculty is both friendly and helpful. On the downside, the students go on to say that during their first week at our school the large building was intimidating and they became lost a few times— but after one week they knew their way around and acclimated quickly. The bottom line is they feel they will get a better overall education at our school and that is why they made the decision to return. However, I do acknowledge that not all public high schools are equal.

The keys to raising successful students who enjoy high school are the same no matter which school parents select. Students need:

- a close relationship with a special circle of friends
- effective study habits
- to get involved in extra-curricular activities, and
- to stay out of trouble with the school administration, parents, and law enforcement personnel.

Start laying the groundwork for your child's freshman year during the eighth grade, if not sooner. If you have not already done so, begin attending some of the activities at the high school. Try to get your son or daughter, along with some of his or her friends, to join you for football games, basketball games, concerts, and school plays. When these activities have concluded consider inviting everyone, including the parents of your children's friends, back to your home for socializing. High school athletic departments sell season passes for reasonable prices which makes getting involved easy and economical. The more parents and their middle school students attend high school functions, the more comfortable they will be when they start as full-time students.

Pay attention to newsletters sent home by the schools. An eighth grade orientation night will probably be held sometime in the spring. Whenever your school offers this program, I would encourage you and your eighth grader to attend. During the spring many public high schools in our city now offer open houses to the families who reside within their districts. Competition for students between public and private schools is increasing and open houses can give parents and students an opportunity to make objective comparisons. Some high schools are also offering incoming freshmen an additional summer orientation program designed specifically for the student. Ours lasts as long as a typical school day and is run by upperclassmen and faculty. Many freshmen tell me this program has been a big help in making the beginning of high school go as smoothly as possible. Upperclassmen and the school itself become less intimidating, which contributes to a higher comfort level. Finally, students should make sure all necessary paperwork for school registration is completed; having a parent along to assist in the registration process is a good idea for the freshman year. The first week of high school is challenging enough for most new students. They should not have to worry about a paperwork glitch resulting from improper registration.

I cannot overemphasize the importance of friendships during the high school years. Parents can help nurture their children's relationships or make them more difficult. My wife would occasionally remind me as the kids were growing up and when I started to complain about activities I did not want to be involved, "Remember Jack, we're making memories." Keep in mind that students get only one chance at high school. In these four years they make memories for a lifetime; upon graduation they will see them as having gone by very quickly. It seems as though one day we parents are attending a high school freshman orientation and the next we are wiping tears from our eyes as we drive home from the dorm after saying goodbye to our college freshman. I remember shaking my head and wondering, where did the time go? **Make the most of these special times because you will not experience them again.** Try to live life with your kids in such a way that when they leave home you have few regrets.

An inviting home is important to enable parents to create the kind of environment that makes kids want to visit. Money spent on pizza, snacks, and soft drinks is well worth the cost in the long run. We were fortunate to have a basement where the kids could hang out. We had a refrigerator downstairs and stocked it full of different soft drinks so guests could just help themselves. Popcorn, pretzels, and other bags of snacks were on the counter next to the refrigerator. There was a game table, cards, Ping-Pong table, and television with a VCR/DVD player. Be realistic and understand that more teenage guests means accidents are bound to happen. There will be spills every once in a while, something might get broken, and it might be wise to pick a color other than white for your carpets. **Within reason**, do not get upset over a little mess. Be respectful and friendly to your children's friends and learn their names. When you meet kids you do not like try to be as tactful as possible on the subject. I think you will find that your kids will figure out for themselves what you wanted to tell them.

If you decide to host a larger party realize that not all of the neighbors will be enthusiastic. When our daughters were in middle school they started a routine that grew bigger each year. The girls built a fire pit in the back yard. Our home is located within walking distance of the high school stadium and after attending home football games on Friday nights, a few friends would come back to our house for a bonfire. The kids would make s'mores, roast hot dogs, and enjoy each other's company. By the time our younger daughter had reached her senior year a few friends had grown into more than one hundred friends. We also invited any interested parents to join us. This was a good opportunity to get to know the parents as well as to have plenty of chaperones. The bonfires were a lot of work, but the kids had a lot of fun.

In the fall, a few days before the first home football game, our younger daughter came up with a good idea for communicating with our neighbors. She typed up letters informing them about what was going on and then hand delivered them. She included in the letters the dates of the bonfires, her name and phone number so they could express any concerns, and a promise that on Saturday morning she would pick up any trash left on the street or in their yards. These letters were well received by our neighbors. I am guessing they were not thrilled about cars parked up and down the street on Friday nights and they probably did not appreciate the extra trash. However, they were informed ahead of time and they knew our daughter would be there on Saturday morning to clean up. Hosting those parties helped make a lot of memories for a lot of kids. When they get together and reminisce about high school I have overheard them talk about how much fun they had at those bonfires. Activities such as these can bring kids and their parents closer together and helps nurture friendships that carry over into the school week and enhance the whole experience.

As a teacher and parent I have observed three critical times during which friendships can be seriously affected. The first potential change occurs when students move from elementary to middle school. The security of childhood and elementary school friendships can be threatened as their social activities expand. Secondly, changes occur as kids make the move from middle to high school. Eighth and ninth grade will often confront students with that proverbial fork in the road and force them to decide which way they are going to go. Some students make the wrong choice and are drawn to excessive partying, sexual promiscuity, smoking, drinking, and other forms of drug abuse. The lives of students who choose the right direction are also disrupted as they watch old friends who make the wrong choices break away to socialize with new friends. The kids on the right track feel sad, worried, disappointed, abandoned, and angry as they see what is happening to people they have grown up with and still care about. The third time of change is when students get their driver's license. They will then have more independence than ever before and parents will no longer be needed for taxi service to and from their activities. Without adults around to supervise them the party groups use this newfound freedom to pick up the pace.

We knew these changes were happening to some of our daughters' friends because we did not see these particular kids at our house anymore. I had become used to having their friends come over and then, suddenly, they were no longer around. When I inquired as to the whereabouts of specific friends, the girls usually answered with something like, "Oh, she hangs out with different people now," or, "She just has some different interests now, Dad." I could tell this loss of old friends upset our girls but they got over the hurdle and moved on. As some of the old crowd disappeared new friends started showing up and were welcomed into our home. Parents who develop a close and trusting relationship with their children might want to remember that if they do not really want to know the answer to their question, they should not ask it. Effective parents learn to read between the lines so everything does not have to be spelled out for them. Kids appreciate this ability.

One piece of advice we gave our girls that seemed to help was, "Just because your old friends are caught up in activities you aren't comfortable with, try not to pass judgment on them. Their choices don't necessarily make them bad people. They may be making bad decisions but **don't burn your bridges with old friends.** You shouldn't get involved in what they're doing, but try not to destroy the relationship by saying or doing something you might regret later." We also told them that time has a way of taking care of problems. Once some adolescents get through the party phase they often get their priorities back in order. If that happens, old friendships can be renewed and be picked up where they were left off.

Having daughters changed the way I relate to females. Even though I had sisters, aunts, cousins, friends, grandmas, a mother, and a wife, after the birth of our daughters my outlook towards women evolved. When I thought of my girls many of the female jokes I had laughed at in the past did not seem quite so funny anymore. Although I had always believed in equal rights for women I did not intend to help raise a couple of liberal feminists. However, I did expect our daughters to grow up to be assertive, confident, and classy, and to have a career of their own choice. My improved awareness of the needs of females carried over into how I dealt with our girls in dating situations.

During sixth grade our daughters' circle of friends was predominantly female but on occasion would include boys. By eighth grade the pattern had reversed itself and the group was usually coed with an occasional all-girls gathering. This situation continued into their high school years. We preferred this arrangement and encouraged it. By socializing in groups, boys and girls find it easier to meet and get to know many different kids in a relaxed and informal setting. During the year the schools occasionally held big dances. In middle school the main social event was the Valentine's Day Dance and the eighth grade dance. In high school, the Homecoming Dance and the Prom were considered highlights on the social calendar. Our girls, along with many of their friends, would have dates for these special occasions. I remember them saying they usually had more fun at the other dances and events when they were not committed to being with one date for the entire evening.

I have known teens who believe they need to pair off and always have a steady boyfriend/girlfriend. Some feel inadequate or insecure if they are not dating someone. Some parents also worry that something is wrong with their teenage son or daughter if he or she is not in a dating relationship. During their high school years I was always much happier to see our daughters socialize in groups. I really did not want our girls to have a steady boyfriend because we had fewer worries that way. When kids get involved in a serious dating relationship they have a tendency to isolate themselves from the rest of their friends. The new couple may prefer spending time alone together rather than with their friends. Old friends miss them and this can cause hard feelings that are difficult to mend once the exclusive relationship has ended. Teenagers should not jeopardize lifelong friendships over short-term romances.

Earlier I discussed the decision-making process for kids. In fourth or fifth grade parents should have initiated their discussions on sexuality, including the difference between love and infatuation. It is also the time to warn their children of the risk of teenage pregnancy and the tough times that follow such a mistake.

In addition, I asked our daughters to avoid putting their mother and me in the position of being grandparents before they were married and could provide for the needs of their babies. I went on to say that I did not think it should be our responsibility to raise our grandchildren. We would love to baby sit the grandchildren but not raise them. **That was their job, not ours.** I told them at this point in their lives they did not have the financial resources to fulfill the responsibility of providing for the needs of a baby. I discussed with our girls how much money is involved in taking care of children. I wanted them to understand that it was our choice to have two children and that we enjoyed raising both of them. However, as the time was approaching when we could refocus our investments on their college educations and a comfortable retirement, we did not want to be put in a position where we would be expected to financially support our grandchildren as well. **I pleaded with them, "Please don't do that to me and your mother."** The girls could tell by my facial expressions and tone of voice I was very serious and meant every word. I confided that either one of them having an unplanned pregnancy or getting involved with drug abuse were my biggest fears as a parent.

Having a baby should be one of the most important events in a man and woman's life. The hardest and most challenging job I know of is being an effective parent. For my wife and me it has also been the most rewarding job we have ever had. Parents must instill into their children the importance of family. If they do not, how will their children know how to create their own family? Almost one in every three babies born today is illegitimate. That, to me, is a frightening statistic. In my high school, I frequently notice unplanned pregnancies. Listening to the students talk, one would think the teenage mothers are acquiring puppies, not having babies. Their poor attitude is a result of poor parenting. **Having a baby is a huge responsibility!** This understanding must start long before high school.

After parents have done as much as they can to anticipate possible problems there may be more work for them to do. When they conclude that their teenage son or daughter is involved in an ongoing relationship that shows no signs of breaking up, I believe another serious discussion is called for. During the sex education unit I teach at our school I bring up the topic of abstinence throughout our discussions. I emphasize abstinence in our sexually transmitted diseases unit. Students tend to be more receptive to the concept at this point. Learning about the latest research on STDs should be enough to put a stop to teenage sexual promiscuity. *It has not.* In spite of comprehensive sex education programs that emphasize abstinence, about one million teenage girls in our country become pregnant every year. I advise my students they have two choices. Either do not have intercourse or, if they do, use effective birth control. I re-emphasize the abstinence option. Unfortunately, too many students choose a third option; intercourse with no contraceptives. A fourth option has been increasing for middle school and high school students: oral sex.

Oral sex is an issue that needs to be addressed when discussing sex education with kids. Students tell me that for a growing number of teenagers oral sex is as common as a kiss goodnight at the end of a date. This is usually a one way street with the girls performing oral sex on the boys. I was asked by a student whether a girl who performed oral sex on a boy is still considered a virgin. Before I answered the question I wanted to hear what the class thought. Almost every student said they believed the girl would keep her virginity. When the students had expressed their views I began to answer the question by saying that if one applies the standard definition of a virgin, because the girl did not have intercourse, technically she was still a virgin. I went on to say that what we were actually talking about is intimacy. There is a big difference between having sex and making love. Making love is something that should be very special between two people who love, respect, and are committed to each other. In my opinion, if a teenage girl performs oral sex on a boy she is no longer a virgin. Whether it is intercourse or oral sex, both are intimate acts, and I do not differentiate between the two other than in the potential for conception.

I could sense many of the students, especially the boys, did not agree with me. I singled out one of the more outspoken boys to help make my point a little clearer. I repeated his earlier comment that oral sex is not any big deal and definitely not in the same category as intercourse. I continued, "Let's fast-forward a few years. You are twenty-eight years old and falling in love with a woman you think you may want to marry. She invites you to her ten-year high school reunion. You have been at the celebration for a while and many of the guests have had a few drinks as they socialize with old friends. You go to the bar for a beer and a couple of your girlfriend's old classmates start up a conversation. It seems they think you're the luckiest man in the room. When you ask them why, they tell you all about the woman you think you're in love with. They remember all the details and take great delight in sharing them. You find out she performed oral sex on just about half the boys in her class and many of them are at the reunion. You begin to notice some of those men giving your girlfriend knowing glances when they don't think you're paying attention." I ask my outspoken male student, "Do you think you would still want to marry the girl who performed oral sex on half the football team?" He begins to feel the eyes of the girls in our class glaring at him. As he thinks about my question he seems a little unsure of himself. He finally says in a quiet voice, "Probably not." I follow up by pointing out that she did not have intercourse. Using his words I ask, "But it was just oral sex. What's the big deal?" Having or not having oral sex is not the main idea. The point is that both oral sex and intercourse are intimate acts which should be between two people who love each other. Furthermore, teenagers need to understand that in today's society, sexuality needs to be within a mutually monogamous relationship with an uninfected (STDs) partner. Unplanned pregnancies, STDs, and emotional problems that can result from doing too much too soon can develop in sexually active teenagers. Some will say, "I never thought that would happen to me." Unfortunately, these problems are happening at an alarming rate to a lot of young people.

This exchange opens up an opportunity to raise a few more important points with my class. Sex has always been subject to a double standard. Males who have sex with numerous partners are seen by many as cool, studs, or players. When a female does the same thing her reputation is damaged. She will be looked down upon by many and have terms like slut or whore associated with her name. The females who have sex with many different males will probably have trouble getting any of those same men to marry them. The men are perfectly willing to use and abuse a female but do not want to marry a woman who behaves in that way. I try to get my female students to understand that performing oral sex or having intercourse with a boy or man is not going to make him love and respect her. **Girls also need to know that oral sex can spread STDs.**

A senior high school athlete attended a party during the summer. While at the party he met a girl who ended up performing oral sex on him. After the party he did not see the girl again. The girl at the party had appeared much older but was actually a seventh grader at the middle school. The same girl started bragging to some of her middle school friends about performing oral sex on the high school's star athlete. News such as this travels quickly through the school grapevine. Eventually the girl's father found out about the incident and he was furious. In October, the father was in the principal's office at the high school demanding something be done to this athlete. The principal suspended the athlete from the team. In addition, even though the oral sex was consensual, since the young man was eighteen years old, the father announced he was going to press charges against the senior boy. Suddenly oral sex became a very big deal. This incident was frustrating and embarrassing to all the people involved.

The next few questions I ask my class elicit a spirited response. If a couple decides to have intercourse, whose responsibility is it to prevent an unplanned pregnancy, the boy or the girl? Most of the class agrees that both partners should share in this responsibility. My next question is: if a couple decides to have intercourse, who risks the most, the boy or the girl? At this point we are focusing on an unplanned pregnancy; I discuss the emotional aspect of this issue at another time. The discussion on this question invariably has a positive effect for those female students who had never seriously thought about the issue before. They begin to realize that the boy/father runs relatively little risk. Yes, the courts will rule he must pay child support each month but deadbeat dads are a serious problem. Just because our laws require fathers to pay child support does not mean they will do so. To prove my point a number of students tell sad stories about their own deadbeat dads and the hardships they have experienced. Some of the more outspoken girls say they would get a lawyer and go after the father of their child. I try to make them aware that the police and courts have so many cases that the pursuit of a disobedient father will be way down on their list of priorities. The reality is that the teenage girl/mother has much more at risk than the teenage boy/father.

I ask the students about the specific risks to a teenage girl who decides to have intercourse and becomes pregnant. They respond that: she is the one who gets pregnant and carries the baby for nine months, has morning sickness, gets stretch marks, and goes through labor; she is the one who has to endure the birth process. After the baby is born the mother usually ends up with responsibility for the majority of childcare with whoever else she can get to help her with the unending responsibilities. I have observed that most teenage fathers do very little to care for their babies in comparison to the mothers. Once again, students can illustrate the point from their own experience and the girls begin to understand my message. In a perfect world both partners would share in preventing an unplanned pregnancy. In the real world, the female has much more at stake so she better make sure she is proactive in preventing an unplanned pregnancy. In conclusion, **"Better yet, at this point in your lives, take a closer look at abstinence and use some common sense. If you don't have intercourse, you don't have to worry about getting pregnant in high school."**

Another issue facing all teenagers today is date rape. Parents should discuss this topic with both teenage boys and girls. Boys need to know that no matter what a girl says or does beforehand, if she says no to sex he'd better back off. Once a young man is charged with rape, even if he is innocent, the situation can get very ugly. Some sources say that as many as one out of every four females will be raped at some point in their lives. Typically, they are raped by someone they know. Girls need to be careful when they go out on a date; they need to avoid letting down their guard. They need to be observant and alert to prevent their date or someone else at the party from slipping a date rape drug into their drink.

Coed slumber parties are popular in our area. Some parents think these activities are innocent and nothing to worry about. I disagree. In this day and age, teenagers are being exposed to more and more situations they are not ready to handle. Our society is getting to the point where it appears that almost anything goes. The kids are becoming desensitized to sex at a younger age which contributes to the inappropriate sexual behavior we see in our middle and high school students. We would not allow coed sleepovers to be hosted at our house. We decided against providing the kind of environment that invites poor decision-making.

We expected our daughters to have jobs during the summer. Starting with the transition between sophomore and junior year of high school, the girls worked the equivalent of a forty- hour week through each of their summer breaks. **This still left plenty of time for them to have fun with their friends.** If students plan their schedules properly and make good grades during the regular school year, summer school is unnecessary after the sophomore year. I believe the benefits derived from working in the summer will help kids in several ways. My students roll their eyes at this and tell me that summer is the time for fun. My students make comments such as, "Why do you think the time is called summer vacation? If I am on vacation, I am going to relax and have some fun. I'm not going to work for minimum wage. You can't expect me to work at some boring job all summer." These spoiled kids should not be permitted to maintain this lazy attitude. The same parents allow their children to do nothing yet continue to give them what they ask for, including money.

I believe working during the summer can help motivate kids to get their education. During my high school years I worked at a car wash and, as I wiped off my side of the car, I remember looking across the hood at my 46-year-old partner. I was beginning to seriously think about my future. I was a teenager and yet this older man was doing the same job for the same minimum wage. I remember thinking I did not want to be working like this when I was his age.

When parents expect their kids to work it also helps them learn the value of money. If parents *give* their teenagers everything they want, how can they expect the kids to appreciate anything? Working summer jobs also helps children learn the necessary skills to work successfully with other people. They must get along with a boss and co-workers. A whole new set of people will relate to your child every day and he or she will learn to better adapt to different situations. In short, working at a full-time summer job is an education in itself.

We made a deal with our kids during their freshman year of high school. We agreed to pay for their four-year college education at a state school. This would include tuition, books, room and board, and sorority fees if they decided to affiliate. With this arrangement, they could graduate from college debt-free and move on with their careers. They would, however, be expected to pay for anything else they needed or wanted. The "anything else" can add up to a great deal of money. Such a plan forces the students to think about how they spend money because they must budget their finances over four years of college. At college, both girls understood they were not to call us for money unless there was an emergency. We decided together that they should each aim to have four thousand dollars in their savings account by the time they left for college. This arrangement has worked well for our family. Our daughters also had worked hard *toward* college before they arrived on campus. They understood our commitment to their education and we knew they were committed as well. This mutual understanding builds strong ties.

We also gave our girls a few tips concerning their summer jobs. For most kids the jobs are not much fun and can get boring. We told them when their boss offered them the job it was they who agreed to take it. They should consequently give an honest effort, try to carry out what their boss expected, and have a good attitude. When the time came to quit we advised them to give their boss two weeks' notice and to try to leave on good terms. When interviewing for their next job, the potential boss may ask about their last place of employment and may contact their former bosses. The kids would want them to give positive recommendations. Teenagers need to have these ideas explained; do not assume your children understand these concepts.

Although we expected our children to work full-time in the summer, during the school year we preferred them to undertake very limited part-time work. Most kids will need to work for the rest of their lives. Students only get one chance at high school. During the school year the teenagers' number one priority should be school and school activities. We did not want our kids rushing off at three o'clock to some minimum wage, part-time job. We wanted them to get involved with different activities of their own choosing and have some fun. On Saturday or Sunday they could undertake some part-time work to avoid spending all the money in their savings accounts. Eating dinner together as a family is important but that is impractical if the kids are working part-time jobs until nine o'clock. We tried to emphasize the concept that Sunday through Thursday were school nights. If they had school the next day, after supper we wanted them in their rooms focusing on their homework and to getting to bed at a decent hour. We wanted to do all we could to make their school experience the number one priority in their lives.

As soon as students get their driver's licenses most want their own car. We can all relate to this new desire for transportation and independence. Lyla Fox, a high school English teacher in Kalamazoo, Michigan, wrote an article on this topic for *Newsweek* magazine, titled "Hold Your Horsepower." She wrote:

> "When students go to work for a car, their positive attitude frequently disappears. A job and car payments are often a disastrous combination. These kids are selling their one and only chance at adolescence for a car. Adults in their world must help them see what their children's starry eyes cannot: that students will have the rest of their lives to own an automobile and pay expenses.

Families who can afford to buy a car for their children have the best of both worlds. For others **a compromise needs to be worked out.** The arrangement will be important because unless the deal is fair many teenagers will eventually become frustrated and say, "The hell with it! If my parents are going to hassle me about all this, I'll get a job and go buy my own car." That is exactly what many kids do. I have talked to students who have chosen this option and in some ways I admire them. They go to school from 7:30 a.m. to 3:00 p.m. After school they work at part-time jobs from 4:00 until 9:00 or 10:00 p.m. When they return home from work they try to do their homework. On weekends they work eight to ten hours a day. As a result of this grueling schedule they do succeed in making their car and insurance payments along with the maintenance and gasoline expenses. However, as time goes by, this hectic lifestyle takes its toll.

Students do not have time for extra-curricular activities. Attending school full-time and working so many part-time hours can be a disastrous combination. **Such kids may pay for their cars but they usually do not enjoy high school.**

When I was in high school I did not have a car of my own and neither did most of my friends. We worked out yet another compromise with our parents, one that might still work for today's parents who cannot afford to buy cars for their children. We took turns borrowing our parents' cars and carpooled. My parents permitted me to use their car a couple of times each month. I had five or six friends in the same situation and, by working together, we usually had transportation to wherever we wanted to go. For the most part my friends and I all got along with our parents. A positive relationship is important for this arrangement; otherwise parents will be less likely to trust their kids with the family car.

We were able to purchase reliable used cars for both our daughters. While these cars certainly were not the vehicles of our daughters' dreams, they provided transportation and in turn independence for our kids. Both girls appreciated the freedom, took care of their automobiles, and experienced the delayed gratification of purchasing a new car. At this time parents need to sit down with their kids and explain how car insurance works. Most students in my high school classes have no idea about premiums and deductibles. The rookie driver needs to understand that if he or she causes an accident, the car insurance premium increases significantly. If the teenager gets a ticket for speeding the premium may increase. Students who make good grades may be eligible for a reduction in premiums. Our insurance agent also explained all this to our daughters and I believe hearing it from him reinforced the idea that driving a car is a serious responsibility. Accidents can happen but kids need to be taught to be as careful as possible when they are behind the wheel of an automobile.

As students progress through high school they need to start thinking about their future plans and what they will do after the commencement ceremony. Through this whole process, parents should keep in mind John Madden's advice about enjoying each level of education. College is not for everybody but if kids do not plan on attending college they must consider what they will do after graduation from high school. **The future belongs to those who prepare for it.** I believe strongly in the importance of goal-setting.

The freshman and sophomore years of high school are the time when students become accustomed to, and learn their way around, their new surroundings. Juniors and seniors can be a little intimidating. When your children are just beginning, do not expect them to seriously consider life after high school. **Freshmen need to focus on getting off to a good start.** Many of the ninth graders I deal with do not understand that poor grades in the first year make it difficult for them over the following three years to raise their grade point averages. I have heard upperclassmen say they wish they had taken their grades more seriously from the first day of ninth grade. They make good grades as juniors and seniors but failed to apply themselves as underclassmen. As a result, their class rank and G.P.A. are not nearly as high as they could have been. As students enter the spring of their sophomore year they will plan their schedule for junior year. That is a good time for them to start taking a closer look at what they want to do following graduation.

Students can be categorized into three basic groups. The members of one group plan on attending college and think they know what they want to major in. The members of a second group plan to attend college but they are not yet sure what they want for a career. Members of the third group are not going to a traditional state or private college. For many students the junior year of high school can be the toughest. This is particularly true for college-bound students because of the limited number of electives combined with upper level classes in: Math, English, Science, History, and Foreign Language. High school juniors usually fill out their remaining schedule with one, or possibly two, electives. There are several more openings for electives in their senior year. During junior year the students who know what they want to study in college need to start investigating which colleges are strong in their areas of interest. Parents should consider visiting the universities that qualify with their son or daughter. While they are there they should ascertain from the admissions office the entrance requirements and important information such as the required S.A.T. score, grade point average, class rank, any required courses for their senior year, cost, scholarship and financial aid opportunities. While this can all be done through the mail or the internet, an on-site visit is preferable. When student and parents have gathered all the necessary information they can set goals and formulate a plan to meet those objectives.

In an ideal world all high school students would know what they want to study in college. In the real world that is not the case and such indecision is common, if not normal. We cannot force kids to sit down and decide what they want to do with the rest of their lives. Eventually most students figure it all out. Some kids who think they know exactly what they want to study in college later change their minds and switch majors after a few semesters at their university.

For high school students who want to go to college but are unsure about their career choices, I have a few suggestions. They should take a variety of electives, particularly during their senior year. It is possible one of those classes will spark a new interest. They should maintain a good G.P.A. so that when they do make a decision poor grades and a low class rank will not hold them back. They should take their S.A.T. seriously. Most kids in our area take the test in the spring of their junior year. Before my daughters took the S.A.T., I borrowed a tape from our guidance department that contained excellent advice on taking the test. I am sure most high school counselors have access to similar tapes and would be willing to permit their students to borrow them. In some locations high school students can take a private class to help them prepare for the S.A.T. The internet can also be a source for additional information. Like good grades and class rank, a good S.A.T. score will enable your child to have better options.

If a student is still unsure about career plans in the first semester of his or her senior year there is no need for parents to panic. Schedule a meeting with your child's high school counselor or career planning center. Our daughters benefited from talking to a private psychologist who specialized in career planning. The girls spent about three hours completing a personality survey. A few weeks later they returned to have him interpret their responses and offer advice. I must admit to having doubts about this whole process. I was pleasantly surprised. The psychologist was knowledgeable and his advice was sound. He also gave us a tape of the session to enable us to review his advice if we wished. Most importantly, his objective opinion was well received by our daughters. Parents should also remember that the first year of college is basic, comprising general classes that all students are required to take to graduate. During the second year most classes are directly related to a major. Hopefully, by then the student will have a better idea of the direction in which he or she is headed.

According to the Census Bureau, on information compiled in the year 2000:

> "Someone whose education does not go beyond high school can expect to earn about $1.2 million for full-time work from ages 25 to 64— a typical work-life period, according to demographers. Graduating from college and earning advanced degrees translate into much higher lifetime earnings: an estimated $4.4 million for doctors, lawyers and others with professional degrees; $2.5 million for those with a master's degree; and $2.1 million for college graduates."

If high school students do not plan to attend college they need to start making plans for what they intend to do. Some of my former students have joined the military. Several made careers of this opportunity while others fulfilled their commitment and then took advantage of the G.I. Bill to earn college degrees. The larger high schools have programs to assist students who want to learn a trade. Interested students should take advantage of these programs. In the past, the non-college bound graduates could get manufacturing jobs and earn enough money to have comfortable lifestyles. Today, many of those jobs have been outsourced to foreign countries where the price for labor is much cheaper than here in the United States. The opportunities are now in service-related fields. There is a large demand for people who are honest, reliable, and skilled in the service they provide. Mechanics, plumbers, electricians, carpenters, heating and air-conditioning specialists, office personnel, lawn service workers, and painters have all the work they can handle **if they are good at what they do.** A teacher friend roofs houses, builds decks, and constructs screened-in-porches during the summer. People appreciate hard workers and many of his jobs are referrals from satisfied customers. He never advertises yet has to turn down clients. The jobs are so plentiful he does not have enough time to complete them all. If he wanted to quit teaching he could make a good living in his service jobs. Quality child-care is sought by working parents. Our hospitals are facing a critical shortage of nurses and other health care specialists. Whenever I dine out I notice the large number of people who rarely eat at home anymore. Opportunities will be available for students interested in the food service business.

By junior year students need to start setting some specific goals and begin working towards achieving them. I have used several old sayings with kids to get them thinking about the future; perhaps one or two will work for you:

- plan your work and work your plan
- failing to plan is planning to fail, and
- prior planning prevents poor performance.

At some point during high school parents need to teach their kids how credit cards work. Credit card debt has become a serious problem for many college students. College-age students are sent applications for credit cards at an alarming rate. Current information estimates undergraduate college students have an average credit card debt of around $2,700. Incurring this level of debt is irresponsible and unacceptable. Parents must start early and get the jump on credit card companies who circle like vultures around these ignorant and sometimes irresponsible young adults. In addition to credit cards, students need to gain an understanding of debit cards, checking accounts, and savings accounts.

High school is the last level of child development where parents can make a substantial difference. Once their children leave home for college or other pursuits, parents assume the role of advisors. If the young adult does not ask for his or her parents' advice they would be wise to keep quiet. I find this much harder in practice than I expected but I am learning. During the frustrating moments I take comfort from Mark Twain's remark and remember they will not be teenagers forever. When kids leave home after high school they will have more freedom than they have ever known. A parent's job is to teach them that with increased freedom comes increased accountability for the decisions they make. High school gives parents their last prolonged opportunity to prepare their children for the real world.

Notes for Chapter Eleven
Middle School to High School

Notes for Chapter Eleven
Middle School to High School

There is no greater reward for a well-spent life than to see one's children well-started in life, owing to their parents' good health, good principles, fixed character, good breeding, and in general the whole outfit that enables them to fight the battle of life with success.

—William Sumner

Epilogue

While writing this book, I periodically asked my family to read the rough drafts and offer their opinions and suggestions. Among other things, they were concerned that I was misrepresenting our family. The girls said, "We are not 'Ozzie and Harriet,' 'Father Knows Best,' or 'Leave It to Beaver.' You make us sound like we are this perfect little family." Although everything I have written in this book is true, to this point I have not mentioned many of my mistakes. I am the first to state I am no Ozzie Nelson, Jim Anderson, or Ward Cleaver. Although my family is well aware of this, they have strongly suggested I make this position clear to you, the readers. So, in the interest of fair play and balance, I will cite a few mistakes. Trust me, there were many more. Our daughters chuckle about them now, but when these incidents took place no one was laughing. If given the chance, my wife would probably fill chapters.

Arguing is a form of communication at which our family has become adept over the years. For example, my wife and I once discussed taking our daughters on the train to Chicago for a fun weekend. We made the decision after I found out the Kansas City Royals would be in town to play the Chicago White Sox. One of my former high school athletes was on the Royals team and the game was to be played on Father's Day at the brand new Comisky Park. We made reservations, ordered tickets, and called Gary a week ahead to tell him we would be at his game. He invited our family to come to the stadium early for batting practice. He offered to introduce us to some of the star players, and then take me down to the clubhouse to visit before the game started. We were looking forward to an exciting Sunday at the new ballpark. On Saturday morning we all rode the train to Chicago and spent a fun day sightseeing.

The next day we woke to a beautiful Sunday morning in June and I enthusiastically anticipated another enjoyable day in the Windy City. Enthusiastic is not how I would have described my older daughter's reaction when I tried to persuade her to get up early enough to enable us to get to the ballpark in time. As I became more aggressive with my "encouragement" for her to get moving, Sarah began to react negatively. We intended taking the "El" to the stadium and needed to arrive in time to meet Gary for the pre-game batting practice session. Our arguing began to escalate as we left the hotel and continued throughout the train ride to Comisky Park. The hot, humid weather certainly did not help the girls' overall mood. Everyone was grumbling as we made our way to the stadium. The slower they walked, the angrier I became. As we approached the nearly empty arena I heard Sarah say, "Well, I hope we are here early enough for you, Dad! Happy Father's Day." She was giving me her sarcastic, curled-upper-lip, look and that set me off. I snapped back, "How about we just call this Shithead Day, in honor of you?" When Betsy started laughing, Sarah burst into tears.

In spite of a rough start, we entered the arena with hope for better things to come. I figured the girls would get over our argument when we got down on the field. As we walked down the long row of steps toward the Royals' dugout, I began to get a sick feeling in the pit of my stomach. I could not see a batting cage or baseball player in sight. I had dragged my family out here two hours before the game was supposed to start so they could be part of all these fun activities. The women were already angry with me and it was looking like another trip to the doghouse for dear old Dad. It so happened this was also Shriner's Day at Comisky Park. Batting practice had been canceled and the attendant in the Royals' dugout informed me that Gary's team was still back at their hotel. This was not news I wished to share with my wife and daughters who were sitting in the box seats glaring at me. Not only had I upset all three females, but my plans had gone down the drain. I could not even buy them a hot dog and drink because the concession stands were not yet open for business. So, we sat there and spent the next hour and a half of Father's Day watching the Shriners drive children around the field on golf carts. The Kansas City Royals finally arrived just half an hour before the game was due to start. Gary came out of the clubhouse and apologized, but it was not his fault. He did not become aware of Shriner's Day until that morning and did not know how to get in touch with us ahead of time. We were able to talk with him for about two minutes. It was one of those days when I made things worse by getting into an argument with the rest of the family.

On another occasion, when our younger daughter's seventh birthday was coming up, we were going to surprise her with a new bicycle. Betsy asked if we could celebrate her birthday at Showbiz Pizza with the animal band, skee-ball games, pinball, video games, and a large pit filled with colorful plastic balls where small children loved to jump. We knew how much Betsy was looking forward to this time and quickly agreed to her request. Once again, I thought we were all set for some family fun. When the big day arrived we loaded everyone into the car and drove off, intending to surprise Betsy by stopping at the bicycle store for her to pick out her birthday present. As I slowed down the car and pulled into the bicycle shop, Betsy asked in a worried voice, "I thought we were going to Showbiz; why are we stopping here?" Now, the bicycle store just happened to be next door to a little pub where, on occasion, my wife and I liked to eat. Without thinking I had the brilliant idea of teasing my birthday girl a little bit; I winked at my wife and answered, "We changed our minds, and we are going to eat at Muldoon's." I wish I had noticed my wife shaking her head and rolling her eyes before I finished uttering that unfortunate choice of words. Although my wife always seems to know these things ahead of time, I had no idea Betsy would become hysterical in the back seat. I quickly moved in to recover the situation by reassuring her we were going to the bicycle store *next* to the pub so she could select a new bike for her birthday. I told her over and over that I was just kidding and that we really were going to Showbiz after she had chosen her new bike. Betsy did not appear to hear all this and wailed through her tears, "Showbiz, Showbiz, Showbiz— you told me we were going to Showbiz." I had done it again. I was sure everything was set for some quality family time but I had managed to turn the occasion into another argument.

As the doors and windows of any home are closed, the only people who truly know what goes on are the family members inside. I have made my share of mistakes over the years, have lost my temper, and been involved in numerous arguments. However, our family has always been my top priority and I hope they know how much I love them. Where there is **unconditional love and a willingness to sincerely apologize when mistakes have been made**, things can work out in the long run.

I am continually reminded that life is short. None of us knows what the next day or even hour will bring. Anytime we say good-bye to our family, it truly could be for the last time. When I say good-bye to my wife and daughters, they always say "I love you" as I am walking out the door. Many times this wakes me up and I respond, "I love you, too." I wish I could say that sometimes I initiate these exchanges, but usually I seem preoccupied with where I am going. Luckily, the ladies help me refocus on what is important: **love for family**. I received the following story in an e-mail message from a friend.

Recently, I overheard a father and daughter in their last moments together. The airline had announced her departure and standing near the security gate, they hugged and he said, "I love you. I wish you enough."

She said, "Daddy, our life together has been more than enough. Your love is all I ever needed. I wish you enough too, Daddy." They kissed and she left. He walked over toward the window where I was seated. As he was standing there I could see he wanted and needed to cry. I tried not to intrude on his privacy, but he welcomed me in by asking, "Did you ever say good-bye to someone knowing that it would be forever?"

"Yes, I have," I replied. Saying that brought back memories I had of expressing my love and appreciation for all my Dad had done for me. Recognizing that his days were limited, I took the time to tell him face to face how much he meant to me. So I knew what this man was experiencing.

"Forgive me for asking, but why is this a forever good-bye?" I asked.

"I am old and she lives much too far away. I have challenges ahead and the reality is, the next trip back would be for my funeral," he said.

"When you were saying good-bye I heard you say, I wish you enough. May I ask what that means?"

He began to smile. "That is a wish that has been handed down from other generations. My parents used to say it to everyone." He paused for a moment and looking up as if trying to remember it in detail, he smiled even more.

"When we said 'I wish you enough,' we wanted the other person to have a life filled with just enough good things to sustain them," he continued, and then turning toward me he shared the following as if he were reciting it from memory.

"I wish you enough sun to keep your attitude bright.

I wish you enough rain to appreciate the sun more.

I wish you enough happiness to keep your spirit alive.

I wish you enough pain so that the smallest joys in life appear much bigger.

I wish you enough gain to satisfy your wanting.

I wish you enough loss to appreciate all you possess.

I wish you enough hello's to get you through the final good-bye."

He began to sob and walked away.

Some of the people who read this book will find many ideas and suggestions with which they are already familiar. Such people, like me, were probably raised in homes where these common-sense skills for living were taught and we took them for granted. Most of our friends had parents who shared a similar philosophy toward parenting, so we did not believe this approach was anything special. I never fully appreciated my parents until I became a parent. My mom and dad were good to my siblings and me. I can never pay them back for all they did for us. What I have tried to do is pay them forward. My wife and I have strived to help our children succeed in life in the same way our parents helped us. We hope our kids will do the same thing for their children when we become grandparents.

As a teacher I am frustrated that an increasing number of parents are not instilling effective skills for living in their children. The rules to live by with which my friends and I grew up are not being taught to as many children today. I see at my high school on a daily basis the results of this failure and we also see them throughout our society. **Kids raised without common sense grow into adults without common sense.** I hope future generations of parents will make improvements to stop this disturbing trend.

From Diapers to Diplomas is about raising well-adjusted, successful children; it is not a book about how to raise perfect kids. I am seeing more and more parents place unreasonable expectations on their children. Realistically, how many kids become valedictorian and go to Harvard? How many boys get to be the starting quarterback on the football team? How many girls can say they were prom queen? How many students are elected president of the student council? If these achievements come to your children, they will form the basis for some wonderful memories. However, the objective of this book is to help parents raise children who will become happy, responsible, and productive members of society— children who grow into the type of people you would choose as friends, children you would enjoy having live in your neighborhoods, kids who develop into the kind of students any teacher would be pleased to have in the classroom, children who progress into young adults potential employers will be anxious to hire.

Of course, there are different ways to raise successful children. Not all the suggestions I make in this book are going to work for everyone every time. Thanks in part to our own parents' example, these approaches to parenting worked well for our family, as I hope they will for you. In many ways, the children hold our futures in their hands. Fulfill your responsibilities and be the best parents you can be. Understand that what is the easiest way is not always the best way. Teach them well, let them live their own lives, and hold them accountable for their actions. Most importantly, love them.

If Nothing Else, Remember This…

These are the most important points from each chapter.

Chapter One / The Formative Years

As the twig is bent, so grows the tree.

- During the formative years the majority of a child's personality is formed.
- The parent's influence is most effective during the pre-school period.
- A young child needs a loving, close, and nurturing relationship with an adult who is caring for a minimum number of other children. This caregiver-to-child ratio is important because children should not have to compete with each other for the adult's attention.
- Children need parents to notice the things they do. Kids must believe they are more important to their parents than a new car, expensive vacation or a big house.
- The most important present parents can give their child is time.
- Education begins in the home. Read to your children every day.
- Parents cannot expect their children to follow their advice and ignore their example.
- Stimulate creativity in your children. Watching television should be kept to a minimum. Provide kids with paper, crayons, clay or play-doe, stuffed animals, puzzles, blocks, dress-up clothes, toy cars, and trucks.

- Monitor what children view on television and computers. Protect the innocence of childhood.
- Raising children is hard work. *Both* parents need to support each other in providing for the needs of their children.

Chapter Two / Discipline and Respect

The purpose of discipline is not to punish, but to correct.

- Your children must love and trust you. They need to believe you have their best interests at heart.
- Every child's personality is unique. Parents have to figure out what method of discipline works best with each child.
- Separate the doer from the deed. When disciplining children, do not make it a personal attack. Kids must believe their parents' love for them is unconditional.
- Kids need discipline. If parents do not instill discipline, their children will have trouble succeeding in anything they do.
- Parents ought to work as a team in regard to the discipline of their children. They should present a united approach and, when disagreements occur, work out compromises in private.
- You need to begin applying effective methods of discipline in the formative years.
- No must mean no. Be consistent. Do not give a warning unless you intend to act on it.
- You are not your children's friend, you are their parent.
- The punishment for poor behavior should be fair and proportionate. Strive to attain a balance between being too strict and too lenient.

- Children will most likely be disrespectful to parents who are ineffective disciplinarians. This lack of respect can contribute to a breakdown in the parent-child relationship.

Chapter Three / Chores and High Expectations

Model a strong work ethic. Make your expectations clear and see to it your children live up to them.

- If parents expect children to help with household chores, they must initiate a routine during the formative years.
- Do not avoid dealing with a reluctant toddler by taking the easy way out and doing the child's work yourself. You will then be contributing to the development of a "spoiled brat."
- Parents must *invest* time, love, and energy when their children are young to *reap* the reward of a teenager they can be proud of and whose company they truly enjoy.
- Assign daily chores and adjust expectations according to age levels.
- As kids grow, add weekly jobs to their daily responsibilities. In the beginning, the family should all do their weekly chores at the same time. Young children need to see everyone working together and that each person has a role to play. This fosters feelings of importance, pride, and teamwork.
- When young children are used to obeying their parents, they will have fewer problems in school complying with their teachers' expectations.
- Kids must be taught to like what they do, not do what they like. Expecting children to complete daily and weekly chores helps develop a strong work ethic.

- One of the best things parents can teach their children is how to get along without them.

Chapter Four / Decision-Making and Mistakes

The decisions you make will determine the quality of your life.

- Each person's values will be a significant factor in his or her ability to make decisions.
- High self-esteem helps kids resist peer pressure.
- Parents must teach their children how to make positive decisions.
- Having your children seek answers to these questions can help guide them towards the right decisions:
    1. What are all my options? Who is someone I trust to give me good advice?
    2. Would I want family and friends to know about my decisions? Decisions made with the hope that nobody will find out are usually wrong.
    3. Does the choice I prefer seem sensible and honorable to me? Never mind what my friends say or think; what do I think?
    4. Can I live with myself as a result of my decision? Will I feel guilty? Resentful?
    5. How will this decision affect me? Will anyone else be hurt? What is the likely outcome?
- Applying common sense, parents must ensure their children experience the negative consequences of poor decisions.
- When your child makes a mistake it does not mean you are a bad parent.

- Teach children how to turn a mistake into a positive experience. Have them follow this three-step process: 1. Admit it. 2. Learn from it. 3. Do not repeat it.
- *Experience* is mistakes we will not make the next time.
- The family dinner can serve as an informal forum where parents can enhance their children's decision-making process through discussion of daily events and activities.

Chapter Five / Self-Esteem

Love your children for who they are, not what you want them to be.

- Parents who provide a loving and stable home for their children promote the development of self-esteem.
- Children must be able to love and respect themselves before they can love and respect others.
- During the formative years children need consistent attention and approval.
- Have a sense of humor. Laugh together when your children say or do something funny. Do not take yourself too seriously and have fun with your kids.
- Family videos and photographs are important. Kids like to watch themselves on videos and it helps them become more poised, assertive, and articulate.
- Avoid comparisons between siblings and treat each child as an individual. Encourage your kids to make an honest effort in whatever they do. Help guide them into activities that highlight their strengths.
- The way your children are treated by people outside the family circle will affect their self-esteem.

- When kids sense they are liked and accepted by others they build positive self-esteem. Conversely, if children feel others do not like and accept them it can have a devastating effect on their self-concept.
- Raise your children with good manners. Teach and model the Golden Rule so they will be considerate and kind. Nurture the development of a good sense of humor. Do this and most people will accept and like your children.
- Appearance is important, but character and personality should be the top priorities.
- Progress from unconditional praise during the formative years to complimenting your older child only when he or she truly deserves it.

Chapter Six / How to Raise a Successful Student

The direction in which education starts a man will determine his future life. — Plato

- Kids should be taught to take a personal interest in their own education. When children develop a sense of educational ownership they will become self-motivated instead of parent-motivated.
- Parents must sincerely care about their child's education. There is a link between parental interest and student achievement.
- Parents need to be enthusiastic and actively involved in their child's education.
- When their child is involved in an activity, parents should attend to support their son or daughter. Make the child feel that his or her activity is important.
- Be a supportive but not overly involved parent.

- Avoid living vicariously through the accomplishments of your children.
- When parents choose to be part of a volunteer group they should do so for the benefit of all the children and not to promote their own child.
- Good grades should be a byproduct of effective study habits. Make certain your children are making an honest effort toward their schoolwork.
- Mental toughness will help students succeed in school. Kids must be taught that if they only work on the days when they feel like it they will not accomplish much with their lives. Mentally tough students will get the job done while the others will make one excuse after another.
- If children get in trouble at school they should be in even more trouble at home. When a disruptive student is causing problems all a teacher should have to ask is, "Do I need to call your parents?" This should be enough to get the child's attention and correct the inappropriate behavior.
- Do not allow your child to get away with making excuses. Parents who accept excuses raise children who end up substituting rationalization for performance.

Chapter Seven / Dependability and Commitment

Actions speak louder than words.

- As the number of unreliable people increases so will the community demand and appreciation for individuals who are dependable and follow through on their commitments.

- When people demonstrate dependability others learn to trust them. Without trust, any relationship will experience trouble, if it survives at all.
- As children grow, parents will have opportunities to nurture the development of dependability. Parents should recognize and take advantage of these "teachable moments."
- Parents who raise dependable kids lay the foundation for their ability to make and keep commitments.
- Parents should see to it that their children develop a pattern of following through on their commitments. Quitting should not be an option.
- Determination is an important part of dependability and commitment. Kids who become easily discouraged grow into adults who become easily discouraged.
- When parents over-schedule their children's activities it becomes difficult if not impossible to demonstrate dependability and follow through on commitments. Kids cannot be in two places at the same time.
- Over-scheduling activities can slowly break down the closeness of the family.
- To keep the lines of communication open between parent and child parents must develop the important skill of being a good listener. This takes time and you cannot rush through it. When that time is taken up by over-scheduled activities, communication breaks down and problems can develop.
- As dependable children grow into adults, the ability to make and keep commitments will benefit them in many ways. Their professional and personal lives will be more successful and rewarding.

- Talk is cheap. Unreliable people often end up unhappy and frustrated as their professional disappointments combine with their personal problems.

Chapter Eight / Extra-Curricular Activities

Students should get involved with extra-curricular activities for the reward, not the award. — Eric Clark

- Participation in extra-curricular activities can affect the quality of a student's school experience. When a student makes new friends, feels connected to the school, and looks forward to upcoming events, these positive experiences can carry over to his or her schoolwork.
- As students consider their selection of extra-curricular activities they need to be aware of the level of commitment required for participation (substantial to limited). The expectations will depend on the activity itself and the leadership style of the coach, director or sponsor.
- Students should become involved for the reward, not the award. Parents should support this approach. Students who participate for selfish reasons will probably be disappointed.
- Programs requiring a substantial commitment offer the most potential benefit. These are the extra-curricular activities in which students are being motivated by coaches and directors to levels of achievement they probably would not reach on their own.
- Students in programs requiring a substantial commitment can learn an effective approach to preparing for serious competition. Learning to make a commitment to excellence

can carry over into their adult lives, helping them succeed in whatever they do.

- Involvement with extra-curricular activities requiring a substantial commitment can reinforce the following qualities: sportsmanship, strong work ethic, teamwork, understanding of roles, responsibility, goal-setting, dealing with adversity, paying your dues, mental toughness, loyalty, setting priorities, time management, and not making excuses.
- Many students are not willing to attend structured practices after school every day and do what is required during the off-season to remain on the team. These teenagers are not prepared to sacrifice weekends and vacations for competitions and more practices. Kids who feel this way need to know it is okay and that there are plenty of other activities available that expect a limited commitment.
- Kids need friends to share movies, games, dances, plays, concerts, and all the other everyday things teenagers do. Quality friendships are more likely to develop during extra-curricular activities than in the classroom. These friendships may last a lifetime.
- Students want their parents to attend their games and performances. However, parents should be supportive from a distance and not get overly involved.
- Coaches and directors appreciate parent volunteers as long as they are participating for the right reasons. Some parents become involved to promote their own child. Others try to tell the coaches or directors how to run their programs. Such conduct is unacceptable and counterproductive.

Chapter Nine / Drugs

Your children will be exposed to drugs and you will not be there when it happens.

— Connie Hines

- A teenager who abuses drugs will adversely affect the members of his or her family in some way —physically, emotionally, and financially.
- Involvement with drugs can mean involvement with people who live by a different set of values. It is no coincidence that when drugs are involved violence can be as well.
- Parents must begin the anti-drug message to their children in elementary school and never let up.
- If parents do not sit down and really listen as their children explain how they feel, it is unlikely the kids will be receptive to their advice. As teenagers see it, if parents will not listen to them why should they listen to their parents? Children must know that you care before they care what you know.
- When kids use together, drugs become the common denominator that makes acceptance to the group almost a certainty. Students with low self-esteem can in this way temporarily satisfy the need to fit in.
- Other reasons kids abuse drugs include: poor adult role models, boredom, too much leisure time, rebellion, lack of discipline, curiosity, escape from reality, and a genetic pre-disposition.
- Denial is a major factor in drug abuse. Parents must intervene when they first become suspicious.

- Running a very close second to denial is being an enabler. Parents must hold their children accountable for their own actions.
- Without structure and guidelines, coupled with negative consequences for bad decisions, kids do not feel their parents love them. However, rules without relationship equal rebellion.
- The concept of gateway drugs should be taken seriously. Experimentation with alcohol, cigarettes, and marijuana is a warning sign that must be addressed.
- Parents should ask themselves why they oppose teenage drug abuse. When they are clear in their own minds about the answer to this question, starting in elementary school, they must communicate that message to their children. Learning about the abuse of drugs will allow parents to communicate more effectively.
- It is no coincidence that many teenagers who develop drug problems have suffered through a parental divorce. When parents and children do not successfully deal with divorce, drug abuse is one of several problems that can develop.

Chapter Ten / Elementary School to Middle School

The Awkward Years

- Middle school is a time when kids are trying to determine who they are and where they fit in. Compounding this identity crisis is the realization that middle school is largely concerned with material issues.
- When compared to the elementary years, middle school exposes students to more experiences, both positive and

negative. Adolescents begin making adult-like decisions on their own. This is when parents are no longer at their children's sides telling them what to do, a time when peer pressure is at its strongest.

- The security of neighborhood and elementary school friendships can be threatened as old friends start to expand their social circles to include new faces from other schools. Although cliques take root in fourth and fifth grades, they blossom in middle school.
- When parents notice so-called friends are upsetting their children they need to be good listeners, offer tactful advice, and then let the kids work out the issues among themselves.
- Clothing is important to middle school students. Parents should acknowledge this priority and guide their children to keep the issue in proper perspective.
- Gossip can cause problems in middle school. What kids do not see with their eyes they should not witness with their mouth. Students should try not to say anything behind someone's back that they would not be willing to say to their face or have repeated to that person.
- Parents and their middle school student can begin to drift apart unless parents make an effort to stay connected. Make the evening meal together a priority or the family dinner will slowly disappear.
- The middle school years will probably be tough on students' self-esteem. Puberty causes major changes in their bodies resulting in an intense, self-conscious focus on personal appearance. This physical transformation occurs at the same time that appearance assumes a top priority among many adolescents.

- Envy is the enemy of happiness and often money is the cause. Parents need to demonstrate that success and self-esteem should not be based on how much money people possess. However, money and the family budget are issues that parents must resolve with their teenage children. The middle school years can intensify this potential problem because as kids get older, they get more expensive.
- Part of wisdom lies in knowing what to overlook. Parents must pick their battles with their children wisely.
- The best way to teach children to be more responsible is to give them more responsibility and then hold them accountable.

Chapter Eleven / Middle School to High School

When I was a boy of fourteen, my parents were so ignorant I could hardly stand to have them around. By the time I was twenty-one, I was amazed by how much they had learned in seven years. — Mark Twain

- Children should be aware that although their parents may have been born at night, they were not born last night.
- Trust, but verify. Parents need to respect their teenagers' privacy but be aware of what is going on in their lives so they can be proactive in dealing with the issues that surface.
- The keys to raising successful students who enjoy high school are the same no matter which school parents select. Students need:
    1. a close relationship with a special circle of friends
    2. effective study habits
    3. to get involved in extra-curricular activities, and

4. to stay out of trouble with the school administration, parents, and law enforcement personnel.

- If they have not already done so, parents should begin laying the groundwork for their child's freshman year during the eighth grade. Parents and eighth graders should attend high school athletic events, concerts, school plays, pay attention to school newsletters, attend orientation programs, and go to school open houses. The more parents and their middle school student attend high school functions, the more comfortable the student will be when he or she begins freshman year.
- Live life with your teenagers in such a way that when they leave home you have few regrets. Keep in mind that students get only one chance at high school. In those four years kids make memories for a lifetime; with hindsight, they will see them as having gone by very quickly.
- Creating an inviting home is important so your children and their friends will want to spend time there. Quality friendships are a significant factor in a positive high school experience.
- Friendships may change during the freshman year and again when the teenagers get their driver's license. Parental support is helpful to high school students as they learn to adapt to these changes in their social structure.
- By socializing in groups, teenagers find it easier to meet and get to know new people in a relaxed and informal setting. This is preferable to long-term exclusive dating relationship that has a tendency to isolate the boy and girl from old friends.
- It is not the grandparents' job to raise their grandchildren. High school students must realize that having a baby is a

serious responsibility and most do not have the financial resources to fulfill it.

- Instill into your children the importance of family. Parents who are positive family role models teach their children how to create their own families.
- Following the sophomore year of high school, working a full-time summer job can teach a teenager important lessons he or she would not learn in the classroom.
- If parents cannot afford to buy a car for their high school student, a compromise should be worked out concerning the use of a family car. Working part-time after school and all day on weekends can be counter-productive for a student who is financing his or her own car. Such kids may pay for their cars, but they usually do not enjoy high school.
- When your child begins high school, do not expect him or her to seriously consider life after graduation. Freshmen need to focus on getting off to a good start to their high school years. The end of the sophomore year is a good time to take a closer look at what he or she wants to do following the commencement ceremony.
- Parents need to teach their teenagers how credit cards work. Students should also have an understanding of debit cards, savings accounts, and checking accounts.

Epilogue

This book is about raising successful, well-adjusted children; it is not about how to raise perfect kids. Some parents do not expect enough from their children. Other parents are placing expectations on their children that are unrealistic. The basic objective of this book is to help parents raise children who are happy, responsible, and productive members of society. Children who grow into the type of people you would choose as friends or people you would enjoy living next door to. Kids who develop into the kind of students any teacher would love to have in the classroom. Children who progress into young adults potential employers will be anxious to hire.

About the Author

Combining over three decades of experience as a coach, teacher, and father allows the author to bring a unique perspective to writing a book about parenting. The hands-on knowledge he has gained is immeasurable. Being a teacher has made him a better parent. Being a parent has made him a better teacher.

At the conclusion of the 2001-2002 school year, the author was selected by his peers as North Central High School's Teacher of the Year. Located on the north side of Indianapolis, North Central is one of the largest and most successful public schools in the nation. His school has earned numerous awards at both the state and national levels for achievements in academics, performing arts, and athletics.

Following graduation from North Central High School in 1970, the author attended the University of Evansville. After three years, he transferred to Ball State University where he earned a bachelor's degree. In 1978, he received a master's degree from Butler University. He started teaching and coaching in the fall of 1975 and has spent his entire career with the Metropolitan School District of Washington Township. After teaching at the middle school level for seven years, he transferred to North Central High School in 1982. He enjoyed 25 years of coaching and remains a teacher at the high school. He has been in *Who's Who among America's Teachers* twice. Three times he has been selected by "Top 25" seniors as the teacher who had the most influence on them. The author has been married for twenty-seven years. His wife and older daughter are both elementary school teachers. His younger daughter lives in Chicago working in the field of retail management.

Printed in the United States
54308LVS00001B/145-150

9 781425 943455